LATER

IS TOO LATE

Hard Conversations That Can't Wait

Susan Covell Alpert

Barana Books

The Only Thing Worse Than Talking About Death Is NOT Talking About It

How prepared is prepared ENOUGH? We all know we should be prepared for the future—particularly the inevitable. But how many of us have actually taken that step? We have so many excuses: We're too busy. It's too much work. It's complicated. My partner is taking care of it. It's not my priority. But, in truth, you need to make it a priority or be prepared to face the punishing aftereffects of loss.

Susan Alpert thought she was organized for the future, for the cruel aftermath of the death of her husband of 46 years, but when the time came, she was overwhelmed with paperwork and agonizing decisions. Faced with the shattering truth that her "good planning" was simply not enough, she scrambled through the painful details and logistics of widowhood.

This experience led her to write her successful, autobiographical first book, *Driving Solo: Dealing with Grief and the Business of Financial Survival.* Alpert began lecturing on the practical aspects of grief, meeting hundreds of other women who had learned firsthand about the heartbreaking effects improper preparation have on the survivor. She then embarked on a massive research project, interviewing countless people who had suffered loss from death, divorce, and other upsets. Her findings led to the creation of a preemptive plan, which is presented in this book.

Later Is Too Late is comprised of two parts. Part One is a story-rich narrative detailing the experiences of real women and the wise and heartbreaking lessons they learned, and how you can avoid their pain. Part Two offers a series of easy, user-friendly, step-by-step worksheets to help you navigate your own sequence of preparation, prepare for your own future—and avoid the oversights these women made.

As we learn in *Later Is Too Late*, procrastination is a huge mistake. The time to start is *now*, and this book will help you do just that. A one-stop tool for practical and emotional support, *Later Is Too Late* covers all the topics that must be addressed when preparing for drastic change: household and family responsibilities; legal, financial, civic, and estate matters; the importance of self care; and the myriad of details that are too often overlooked, to disastrous results.

This is the book that will save you and your family from the most stressful and overwhelming work you will encounter when the worst happens. Don't wait; later will be too late.

About the Author

Susan Covell Alpert, author of *Driving Solo: Dealing with Grief and the Business Logistics of Financial Survival* is also a lecturer, entrepreneur, and frequent guest on national radio and television shows. She has been the owner of several multimillion-dollar companies and has impressive experience in the fields of negotiation, finance, international services, and business. She holds a master's degree in psychology and education from Brooklyn College in New York, and most recently devotes her time to consulting and pro bono work in the field of grief and preparing for the future. Alpert resides in Newport Beach and Palm Desert, California.

Later Is Too Late
Hard Conversations That Can't Wait

By Susan Covell Alpert
Copyright © 2016 Susan Covell Alpert

Published by Barana Books

ISBN: 978-1530953851

Library of Congress Control Number: 2016939812

Printed in the United States of America

Cover and Book Design: Patty King
Cover Photo: Adobe Stock Photo/ StockPhotosArt

Dedication

To my amazing family, whose love and laughter pulled me out of my grief, helping me to let go of the past and find hope for the future. I love you Dana and Steve; Bari and Sean; and Jason, Alexa, Matthew, Cade, Hope, and Shane.

PART ONE

Part One Table of Contents

Introduction: And Life Went On... but Not Always as Planned..............17

What You're About to Read..21

A Personal Questionnaire..23

How Did You Do?..26

CHAPTER 1: From Control to Chaos and Back................................29

The Fabric of Life 32

The Hardest Chapter—but Not the Last 35

CHAPTER 2: Stories of Love, Loss, and Success................................39

The Cast of Real People in This Book................................40

CHAPTER 3: A Home Is a House Full of Hope—and Surprises...........45

The Traditional Side to a Modern Partnership 49

A Life Renovation..51

The Bit of Wisdom..52

CHAPTER 4: What You Don't Know CAN Hurt You................55

Almost Is Never Enough..59

Your Unique Estate "Fingerprint"..61

CHAPTER 5: If You Will It, It Will Be...65

Nothing Worth Fighting For..66

Growing Up Fast..68

Roll Up Your Sleeves and Dig Deep..72

A Few Words About Wills and Trusts..73

A Few Words About Executors and Trustees.................................74

A Few Words About Probate 77

CHAPTER 6: The Party No One Wants to Plan.............................77

Preparing for the Inevitable..81

Celebrating Turned to Mourning...84

Have the Tough Conversations Now..86

CHAPTER 7: It's ~~None of~~ All of Your Business 89

The Many Headaches of Loss...90

Hiccup After Hiccup...92

The Most Priceless Gift of All..93

Don't Forget to Tie Up Your Camel...94

CHAPTER 8: The Longer You Wait, the Harder You Fall............97

Facing the Terrible Truth..100

Best-Laid Plans..101

The Comfort of Strangers...103

There Is Only Now...104

CHAPTER 9: When You're the Rock—but You Feel Like a Pebble......107

When the Caregiver Needs a Caregiver...110

The Real Heroes..112

CHAPTER 10: Grieving, but Not Alone.......................................115

First the Shock, Then the Scramble...119

Choosing the Right People Takes Smarts ... and Guts....................120

Who Is Part of Your Support Network?..122

CHAPTER 11: The Fine Art of Reinvention.................................125

In Search of Purpose...128

The Perfect Picture Gets Shattered...129

When Life Gives You Lemons ... Again..131

The Dream Life Unravels..133

Find Yourself Again..136

CHAPTER 12: What Matters in the End......................................139

Secure Your Own Oxygen Mask First...**141**

The "Now" Bucket List...**143**

Lessons Learned the Not-So-Hard Way..**144**

And Life Went On... but Not Always as Planned

"The only way to make sense out of change is to plunge into it, move with it, and join the dance."
~*Alan W. Watts*

If you had told me in 2008 that I would be an author, speaker, and researcher about the business logistics of death, I would never have taken you seriously. Why, of all things, would that even have entered my mind? Why would I choose such a career path at this stage of life, when the world would have me retiring? But the twists and turns of fate often lead us down roads we never considered. For me, what started as a particularly cruel twist suddenly turned into a new and rewarding direction for my life.

August 11, 1962: THE MARRIAGE

January 8, 2008: THE DIAGNOSIS

November 2, 2008: THE DEATH

In the blink of an eye, 46 years passed. Then, one day, my husband Larry and I were blindsided when he was diagnosed with acute myeloid leukemia (AML)—the deadliest form of blood cancer. Although we knew the odds were against him, Larry's boundless optimism and strength, coupled with my own naiveté and overpowering desire to forever hang onto this man I loved, had me in denial. A brief 10 months later, he died, and I was reduced to a shell of the person I had been.

Over the next year and half, I struggled through overpowering isolation, fear, grief, and profound sorrow. I was suddenly a member of a club I never imagined I would join—a club of widows. The emotional journey following the loss of a partner you have loved and laughed and lived with for decades is indescribable and intensely personal. On top of the deep emotional punch, there's the daunting practical task of settling your estate and beginning a new life on your own.

For the first two years, I felt my life was over, that the joyful and useful parts of me had died right along with Larry. But as it turns out, a new chapter was just beginning—one surprisingly filled with happiness, and a purpose all my own. In the years following his death, I circuitously found renewed direction and meaning in my life as an advocate for men and women who had experienced the same deep loss I had.

Five years after Larry's death, I published my first book, *Driving Solo*, in which I chronicled my journey through the grieving process—grappling with both the emotional struggle and the practical aspects of putting my life back together without Larry by my side. *Driving Solo* addressed the bereaved. It was about the pain of loss, the reality of caregiving, the experience of emotional despair, the legal and financial confusion of being suddenly single, and how to climb out of this hole, step by step.

It has been said that necessity is the mother of invention, and *Driving Solo* is a perfect example of that proverb. I never planned to write that book, but there was nothing like it out there (I know, because I looked for just such a resource when I needed it most). The widows and widowers who read it were so hungry for guidance and reassurance from someone who had been through the worst and come out the other side—not exactly unscathed, but more than OK. So, *Driving Solo* was met with an extremely positive response.

Publishing this book opened many amazing opportunities for me to reach thousands of people and share my own hard-earned wisdom about loss. I set off on a national book tour and have since been featured on television and radio, and published and quoted in numerous newspapers and magazines. I've spoken before many diverse audiences and have received letters and compliments from people I've had the great fortune to help in person, those I've never personally met, and those who happened to simply read my book.

What has resonated with me throughout all of this has been the many compelling stories these readers shared with me of their own loss and eventual rebirth. Their intimate words and experiences have stayed with me and were my subconscious inspiration when writing the book you're about to explore.

Despite the inroads I made after publishing *Driving Solo*, and although I was humbled and inspired by the new events in my life, deep down I knew I still had work to do. I knew it in my heart and gut. I just didn't know what *it* was … until I received a call from a young woman who needed answers—not about dealing with death, but about *preparing for it.*

She was worried about her aging parents and what would ensue when they passed. What sort of tasks would she have to add to her already frantic life? What could she do in advance to prevent it from being too chaotic and overwhelming?

She also worried about eventually losing her husband. Rather than waiting for that day and *then* reading my book, she asked what I could recommend for her now. I offered to sit down with her to see how I could help. When we met, I was impressed with her foresight, but had no specific materials to give her. I suggested she modify the manual in the back of *Driving Solo*, download the worksheets from my website, and adapt them all to her particular situation. But she continued to press me: wasn't there an easier way?

The truth is, this was not the first time I had been asked such questions. It seems that every time I've spoken to a group, I've found myself talking about the importance of preparation. While many men and women who read my book, come to hear me speak, and tune in to my media appearances have already suffered a great loss, others are simply curious about what to do *before* the worst happens. Almost everyone fears the unknown, and anything we can do to be prepared for it puts our minds at ease.

That's when it hit me … my "aha" moment.

It dawned on me that while researching *Driving Solo*, I hadn't come across anything that would help men and women prepare for the universal inevitability of loss in a preemptive fashion. Yes, one could find isolated articles and books written by professionals with particular areas of expertise (estate law; grief counseling; financial, legal, and civic management), but in all my exhaustive research, I hadn't found one single resource that combined most everything a person would need to know to prepare for the death of their loved ones or even themselves.

Such a resource—something simple, clear, sympathetic, and personal to the audience—would be an invaluable tool for so many people. It would help them move from the denial of "it could never happen to me" toward a proactive and healthy approach to preparing for loss. It would encourage readers to get around to getting ready *right now*—not when it's more convenient … and possibly too late.

Finally, I realized what I needed to do next. I needed to create that resource. Here was necessity rearing its head again.

Déjà vu: the idea for *Later Is Too Late* was born.

So began my next journey and my new purpose. I once again devoted myself to copious research and writing, but this time, I also added a new dimension. I vowed to "hit the street running," to conduct the bulk of my research with real-live people and not just rely on statistics and facts. I began to talk to others. Many, many others.

My goal was to interview women who had been somewhat prepared for the loss of a loved one as well as those who had chosen the path of denial. I chose to focus on women for this book because women are more likely to be left alone. Women tend to outlive men by about five years, on average.[1] In fact, seven out of ten Baby Boomer wives will outlive their husbands, entering a period of widowhood that can last for 15 to 20 years.[2]

However, it is important to note that *Later Is Too Late* is *universal*. It's for everyone, really: women, men, adult children of aging parents, young married couples with or without children, those responsible for elder relatives or even friends, those living alone. All of these people have one thing in common: the potential to one day find themselves struggling with loss and change, and the desire to make sure they are well prepared for this—dare I say it—inevitability.

What You're About to Read

This book, a sequel of sorts, is in the same genre as *Driving Solo*, and is also a two-part book. Part One is comprised of my own story, along with true tales I've heard from the wide range of women I interviewed. You will read about their situations and the consequences they faced as a result of being prepared (or not!). Each one touched me deeply. Through them, I hope you will recognize some of your own possible scenarios, and discover how to meet them with courage and readiness.

Part Two of this book is a series of interactive, hands-on worksheets, checklists, forms, and practical steps. These materials have been designed specifically for readers committed to taking a proactive approach to

1 Jiaquan Xu, M.D.; Kenneth D. Kochanek, M.A.; Sherry L. Murphy, B.S.; Elizabeth Arias, Ph.D., "Mortality in the United States, 2012," *The Centers for Disease Control*, October 2014. http://www.cdc.gov/nchs/data/databriefs/db168.htm
2 Brian R. Korb, "Financial Planners: Educating Widows in Personal Financial Planning," *Association for Financial Counseling and Planning Education*, 2010, https://afcpe.org/assets/pdf/vol_21_issue_2_briankorb.pdf

planning—people who are willing to get everything together and move forward before it's too late.

There are so many ways we all prepare for the future—investments, retirement funds, college savings, annual physicals, preventative shots—but we shy away from preparing for the one thing that is a truth: the eventual deaths of ourselves and our loved ones. Yet, that is potentially the most important way to ensure our own futures, and the future of our families, when the worst happens.

Before Larry passed away, I thought I had it all together. This book addresses all the ways in which I was prepared for my husband's death, and all those I had not even considered. It's about the lessons I learned and the lessons others shared with me. It's about lessening the stress and anxiety that come with heartbreak. And most importantly, it's about how *you* can prepare, no matter your own unique situation and needs. We all have lessons to learn, and in this case, it's far better to learn from the mistakes and omissions of others than to learn from experience. My hope is that this book will help you do so.

Yes, it can be hard to face the truth that death eventually comes for us all; this makes it challenging to deal with preparation. When you have a free evening, you'd probably rather spend it going out to dinner or seeing a movie than preparing your will, filling out legal forms, and thinking about losing the people you love most. In truth, getting a root canal might even seem like more fun.

But take it from me, the consequences of being unprepared are so much more painful than the preparation itself. Getting ready now will save your time, money, and mental health in the long run. Think about it: you could skip one TV show a week and get started on this instead.

It's easy to procrastinate, but as I and the many women whose stories comprise this book can attest, later is definitely too late.

A Personal Questionnaire

PREPARED ... what does that really mean?

Everyone has a different set of circumstances, so the definition of "prepared" will be different for you than for someone else. But it's important to start with a baseline definition, and you need a tool to get you to that starting point. On the next page, you'll find a quick and cursory inventory list. While you may not have experienced the great loss you fear, I encourage you to complete the questions and ask yourself how you would answer them *if the worst were to happen.*

You can answer this questionnaire about yourself, your partner, a parent, or anyone in your life whom you suspect should be better prepared.

Are you ready? Take a deep breath, pick up your pen, and fill out the worksheet. Keep in mind that this is not for the eyes of others; it's for you and your own peace of mind only. Be objective and honest with yourself. If you can't answer "yes" to most of these questions, then it's time to get more involved in your own future—and the future of your loved ones.

A Personal Questionnaire

1. Do you have an attorney?   YES ☐ NO ☐

2. Accountant?   YES ☐ NO ☐

3. Financial advisor?   YES ☐ NO ☐

4. Do you have a complete list of all your
    insurance policies with names, account
    numbers, and phone numbers of the
    insurance companies holding the policies?   YES ☐ NO ☐

5. Do you have a living will or medical directive
    and does someone have power of attorney?   YES ☐ NO ☐

6. Do you keep records of your medical history
    and a list of your doctors?   YES ☐ NO ☐

7. Do you have all your banking and investment
    documents organized in one place?   YES ☐ NO ☐

8. If you have one or more mortgages outstanding,
    does someone know where to find the paperwork?   YES ☐ NO ☐

9. If you have any rental properties, is the
    pertinent information readily available?   YES ☐ NO ☐

10. Does someone know where to find other important documents such as birth, marriage, death certificates; military discharge documents; social security papers; and passports; as well as all the documents listed above? YES ☐ NO ☐

11. Do you have complete lists of your assets and current liabilities, recurring payments, and three years' worth of tax returns? YES ☐ NO ☐

12. If you have safe deposit boxes or safes either inside or outside your home, does someone know where to locate them and have the combinations and/or permissions? YES ☐ NO ☐

13. If you keep important information or documents on your computer, is it password-protected, and does at least one person know the password and where to find the relevant folders? YES ☐ NO ☐

14. Do you have photocopies of every single credit card, both front and back? YES ☐ NO ☐

15. If you are employed, does someone have contact information for your employer? YES ☐ NO ☐

16. Does someone have information about any active involvement you have in business or social organizations? YES ☐ NO ☐

17. Have you made burial arrangements?   YES ☐ NO ☐

18. Do you have specific requests regarding
    funeral ceremonies, and have you shared
    them with someone who will be in a position
    to make decisions?   YES ☐ NO ☐

19. Have you ever had responsibility and
    experience handling the paperwork for
    a deceased?   YES ☐ NO ☐

How Did You Do?

If the questionnaire left you feeling anxious or even terrified, go ahead and take a deep breath. Throughout this book, I'm going to help you get a handle on exactly what you need to do to be prepared for *anything*. I'll talk about how you can feel in control of the financial, legal, and domestic parts of your life. I'll encourage you to consider all of the unique factors that make your situation yours alone. And I'll illustrate how you will indeed have the courage to go on with your life, no matter what happens.

The purpose of this book is not to frighten you, shame you, or make you worry about the future; nor is it preachy, didactic, or theoretical. Instead it's full of real, in-the-trenches accounts from people who have suffered great loss and made it through.

My goal for this book is to cut down on the extent to which you fear the unknown and help empower you for the future ... whatever it may hold.

CHAPTER ONE

From Control to Chaos and Back

"Death, taxes, and childbirth! There's never any convenient time for any of them."

~ Margaret Mitchell in Gone with the Wind

Two red pigtails hanging down my back, freckles across the bridge of my nose, my father holding my hand as he hugged me before leaving me at my aunt's home for a few hours. I was so little, but still, it's one of the earliest memories I have of my childhood.

What I understood was that everyone was crying because my grandfather had died. I didn't exactly know what that meant, but I knew the laughter and the music—normally a big part of my fun, funny family—had stopped. No one was tickling me; I wasn't giggling. It had to be serious.

That was my first introduction to death. The toll and aftermath on the family was over my head, just the way it was supposed to be, and it stayed that way for many years.

As I grew older, so did my other grandparents, their friends, and their relatives. More tears, more funerals, only now I understood what was happening and attended the services and burials. There were so many, but it wasn't until 1962, two weeks before my wedding, that I truly felt loss in the depths of my being. That was when my father died.

I was crazy in love with Larry, excited about my new life, and suddenly catapulted into reality. Death didn't consider my timing; it had its own agenda. That fact was reinforced when, the following week, my aunt died. Another funeral, more heartbreak, and only six days until the glorious day every starry-eyed girl dreams about.

Despite her own chronic health problems, my courageous and devoted mother insisted the wedding go on. She was radiant on the surface as my brother walked me down the aisle, the epitome of the charming mother-of-the-bride, even when my uncle had a heart attack while dancing and the blast of the ambulance sirens overshadowed "Fly Me to the Moon." Another uncle, suffering from leukemia, had to be assisted out as a result of his weakened condition. One by one, the crowd thinned.

Soon, there were two more deaths in my life, and each time, the music and laughter stopped.

Six months following our wedding, Larry and I received the first of many more late-night phone calls. His father, who had just turned 50, was lying in bed, took a deep breath, and died. This couldn't be happening, but it was. We all went from thinking we were invincible to reeling from shock after shock. In each case, the toll of being unprepared was irreparable.

A few years later, in 1965, we were getting ready for Larry's younger sister's wedding. She was marrying her college sweetheart, and it was to be one of the happier events since my father and Larry's father had both passed away. We were all so excited; even my frail mother was looking forward to the event. Hanging on her bedroom door was the dress she planned to wear to Fran's wedding—coincidentally, she had worn it only once before, at my own. The hair appointments and makeup sessions were scheduled and the cars ordered. Everything was in place. Once again, we naively thought we had everything under control.

Late that cloudy night, the phone rang, startling both Larry and me. It was my brother. My extraordinary mother, only 62 years old, had died. I was in shock; this could not be possible. We rushed over, stunned, and began to make arrangements ... again. The wedding dress hanging on her door became her funeral dress, and it gave me little consolation to know how much she would have liked to think that she was "carrying on" in death even as she had in life.

Larry was at my side during the funeral, looking exceptionally handsome in his elegant tuxedo. Perhaps he was overdressed for the chapel, but he had suited up to give his sister away later that same day. He sped away from the funeral and drove straight to her wedding. Timing has a cruel sense of humor.

I could go on. Life is full of tragedies. We all experience them, but why were they happening with such frequency? As the years went on, we seemed to lose many people dear to us, people of all ages and stages in life, far too often. In 2002, four days before Larry and I were to host an elaborate 40th anniversary party for ourselves at our home, fate once again rudely interrupted our celebration of life and love. Larry's younger sister, only in her 50s, had died suddenly. So young; oh, so young! Larry and I, now in our early 60s, were more accustomed to life and its trials, but Fran's death was still a surprise and hit us hard. It seemed so close to home—Larry's sister, his *younger* sister.

Why am I telling you all this? Not to depress you, and not for pity. I simply aim to remind you that death does not always wait for an appropriate age, nor does it heed a practical timeline. You must prepare for the inevitable, for it will come when you least expect it. We choose to believe that only the old really die, even though we know better. In our protective minds, we believe that death too young only happens to other people. But it will happen to everyone, eventually: you, your partner, your parents and siblings. And if you don't prepare for it, you risk leaving yourself and your loved ones in a terrible position. So many of us mean to get our affairs in order—to organize financial paperwork, to set up wills, to make arrangements for our burials and funerals—but we never get around to it. I'm here to tell you, it's time to get around to it. It's uncomfortable, yes, but it is so important.

The Fabric of Life

Death seemed to be part of the fabric of my life from an early age. Although I was unaware of it then, all of the loss and tragedy I experienced as a young adult were the foundation for the direction my life was to take a full 50 years later. I went through the fire of losing too many loved ones far too young, but I was ultimately able to reinvent myself around my pain in order to help others.

But before I could get to that point, I had to experience my greatest loss of all—my best friend, my lover, my husband.

Larry and I had 46 wonderful years together. Our lives weren't perfect (whose are?), but we raised an extraordinary family and lived happy lives. Our daughters, Dana and Bari—with their husbands, Steve and Sean—gave us six beautiful grandchildren: Jason, Alexa, Matthew, Cade, Hope, and Shane. We were blessed with lots of love and laughter in our lives. Free-spirited entrepreneurs, we were also successful in business and spent decades traveling the world together.

We didn't just love to travel; it was my career. A veteran of the luxury travel industry, I founded a company called International Travel Incentives, which assisted major companies in motivating their teams by rewarding the highest performers with luxury trips to exotic destinations: palaces in Vienna, hot-air ballooning over Paris, meeting with mayors of cities, black-tie dining in the middle of the vast Serengeti. Every trip meant the royal treatment with first-class travel, five-star resorts, and VIP tickets to sold-out events. I had a phenomenal team at the helm, and together we were responsible for dreaming up these fantastic trips, designing the marketing, and producing every moment of the experience.

That meant I did a lot of "research" into the best places to stay and things to do around the globe, often with Larry at my side. Even though he was not an official member of my team, I considered him an indispensable part of my business. With his charm and his zest for life, he was a great travel companion. My clients and staff loved him, and his outside input was of great value.

We traveled together so much that we ran out of room on our passports several times. The adventures brought us even closer, but we were always excited to return home to what I now think of as our beautiful sanctuary. We were surrounded by great friends and always appreciated the luxury we had worked so hard to attain.

Life was good. That is, until Larry's diagnosis in 2008. And so it happened that my knight in shining armor turned out to be mortal after all.

Even after he was diagnosed with acute myeloid leukemia, Larry's outlook on life was always positive. This carried over through rounds of chemotherapy, a bone-marrow transplant, and his ever-declining health. Right up until the last week of his life, Larry was positive he was going to survive, and that certainty was contagious. I never gave up hope that Larry would pull through, and as part of that mindset, I refused to spend much time focused on preparing for him to be gone. But 10 months after his initial diagnosis, gone he was.

While we had known for some time that Larry's condition was serious, I was nevertheless shocked to suddenly be alone. Larry and I had both counted on his recovery, even as the doctors gave us grimmer and grimmer news. We remained positive until the end—and while you might say that was a good attitude for us to have, in many ways it was filled with naiveté.

I was devastated but never questioned what might lie ahead for me from a practical point of view. I was so focused on my emotional state that the logistics of paperwork and signatures seemed unimportant and too painful to face. Life without Larry had no meaning for me, so what was the point of putting the pieces back together? Deep down, I knew I'd eventually have to get through all the forms and filings, and contact the people who needed to be contacted, but I had no way of anticipating the colossal situation I was about to face. It's impossible to understate just how deeply my lack of preparedness affected me later on.

Don't get me wrong; I was probably more prepared for Larry's death than the average wife, at least on paper. Years earlier, before we even knew he was sick, I had taken the time to get our collective finances and legal documentation organized just in case something should happen to one or both of us. I created binders full of instructions for our kids about what to do if they lost both Larry and me, and even sent duplicate binders to my brother and a close friend in New York, in case of an earthquake or other catastrophe. At some point, I had also talked to Larry about where we should be buried (more about this in Chapter 6).

I really thought I was as prepared as I needed to be—almost neurotically so. That's the problem. I didn't know how prepared I needed to be. And sadly, I didn't have anyone at my side to guide me through the process. I was utterly alone. Compounding that, there simply wasn't one place I could get all the information I needed to address my "whole problem."

So it goes that after Larry's death, I spent an agonizing year and a half grieving, vulnerable, stressed out, and overwhelmed. I was faced with decisions that would impact the rest of my life and my whole family. Unless you've been a member of this undesirable club, you can't imagine the difficulty and fear. First, there was the emotional work. Then, there was the paperwork hell as I tried to navigate all the red tape that unfortunately (and somewhat cruelly) surrounds the death of a loved one.

I obviously made it through this period, but it was the hardest thing I have ever done. As a child, I associated death with the end of laughter and music; after Larry died, I was keenly aware that I couldn't remember smiling, laughing, cracking jokes, or tickling my grandchildren for so long. What happened to that humor that had always been part of my life? Boy, did I miss it. I couldn't imagine it would ever return.

Of course, it did. And I came through my personal hell having learned an invaluable lesson: *you must be prepared to lose the one you love the most.*

The Hardest Chapter—but Not the Last

Picture your spouse, your children, your parents, and anyone else you hold dear. What would their lives be like if something happened to you and you hadn't properly prepared your estate and legal documents? What would happen to *you* if you were to find yourself "driving solo"? When we don't prepare for the future, we wittingly cause deep pain, hardship, stress, and desperation for those we love. We cause them to become not just survivors, but victims.

I know this sounds harsh—and it is. It is meant not as a judgement, but as a loving desire to shake you into action.

I like to think my life has been broken up into chapters, just like the chapters of this book. While losing Larry felt like "the end," a new chapter did eventually begin, one with renewed meaning and purpose. In this new chapter, I applied my natural spirit of entrepreneurship to a cause that I feel incredibly passionate about: being a resource for other widows so that they don't have to figure everything out the hard way, as I once did. I created a step-by-step program that gives a comprehensive overview of almost everything that must be done in a simplified, organized, reduced-stress way.

As I took action, my energy shifted from grief and contemplation to drive and purpose. As a result of my own struggle to find answers, I created the Chaos to Control program that led to writing Driving Solo. And I was humbled and filled with gratitude when both the program and book received enormous positive response. But I shouldn't have been surprised.

This resource was so badly needed; people were hungry for direction.

One of the unexpected and amazing rewards of writing and publishing *Driving Solo* has been the many invitations I've received to speak in front of groups. Generally, at these events, I share my story and describe how it set the stage for me to reinvent myself, then offer my advice on how audience members can handle their own varying circumstances. Over and over again, I have found myself standing in front of groups of women and men who do not want to be there. They are there because they need help deciding how to handle what seems like an impossible situation.

Many of the people who attend my presentations aren't dealing with—or even thinking about—the death of a spouse. Instead, they are thinking about different types of losses in their lives: divorce, the responsibility of caring for senior parents or disabled children, living transitions for dependent loved ones, and even how to prepare others for their own deaths. There is always an air of general discomfort in the room when I begin to speak. I hear rumblings of "I don't want to hear this," and "I don't want to be here, but I have to be," and "I'm already prepared enough." I often encounter questions about my credibility, shyness on the part of audience members to speak up, and a generalized reluctance. And almost always, I witness the mood in the room and the attitude of the attendees do a 180 from start to finish. Time and again, I watch as faces go from reluctant to empowered. When I know I have reached my audience, I leave feeling enriched and motivated.

Throughout this book, I'll be presenting lots of hints, caveats, and ideas, but it is all a "wish list" for a perfect world. And as we all know, the world we live in is not perfect. You may not be able to do a flawless job preparing your estate and making a plan, but any inroads you can make and steps you can take will help protect you and your family in immeasurable ways. Don't give up if you don't feel like you can do every single thing I suggest. What's important is to never abandon the process. It's OK to do the work in segments, but make sure you keep going, even if you have to take breaks.

My goal is for this book to make you feel enriched and motivated, not to walk away feeling frightened of all the things that might go wrong. Quite the opposite: I want you to feel empowered and to know that no matter what life hands you, you can handle anything. Because you can. I did, and so did the other women whose stories fill this book.

Even though I still miss Larry deeply and always will, I'm in a great place. Where once I took my husband's presence in our home for granted, now the echoes of my own footsteps in the hall give me comfort. I have learned to stand proudly on my own two feet, and for that, I am profoundly grateful to Larry and to this life.

CHAPTER TWO

Stories of Love, Loss, and Success

"Someone's sitting in the shade today because someone planted a tree a long time ago."

~Warren Buffett

You can talk to all the people in the world, asking for their stories of love and loss, and you'll never hear the same story twice. One of the favorite elements of my work is meeting so many different people, all of whom have led rich lives full of wonder and adventure of one sort or another. I never get tired of hearing their stories, and I am continually astonished by the twists and turns each life has taken.

In all my conversations, I've uncovered only one absolute: *Death is such a traumatizing concept to most people that we don't even like to talk about it.*

Even if we are willing to acknowledge that bad things might happen to us, we prefer to live in denial than to plan for them. But anything can happen, from a long illness to unexpected divorce, from the death of a spouse to the passing of a child or the loss of a parent. Ultimately, we must even prepare for our own demise.

This is our collective reality—a reality I myself embodied when Larry passed away and I witnessed firsthand how important it is to be truly prepared.

For this book, I talked to a variety of women who have suffered their own drastic life changes. I sought out women of all different backgrounds, locations, and ages: the Greatest Generation, Boomers, Gen X-ers, Millennials. Every story was different, every story was real, and every story imparted an important piece of wisdom. The stories of this ensemble cast of characters wrenched my heart, and their bravery inspired me. They are warriors of love, loss, and ultimately, success. In every case, they evolved into strong and capable survivors, but they didn't start out that way. They struggled, they cried, and they felt overwhelmed and helpless at times, but they survived.

Each one touched me deeply. And as you read about these women, I hope you'll take away lessons about how you can protect yourself from the negative experiences some of them had as a result of being underprepared. Others, I hope you'll hold up as role models of preparation. For now, let's just meet the cast of real-life characters in this book.

The Cast of Real People in This Book

Bria

A young mom of 4-year-old twins, her strapping husband Michael died suddenly of a heart attack in his 40s, leaving her responsible for a hefty mortgage in an expensive suburb of San Francisco. A professional go-getter with a demanding job, Bria had always left the domestic work to Michael, and she was baffled about how to move forward in his absence.

Tracy

Married to Chuck for 20 years before he ended his own life in the aftermath of the 2008 banking crisis, Tracy thought she was knowledgeable about the family finances. But while dealing with the shock and grief of losing her husband in such a violent way, she was forced into a painful probate process and ultimately lost her home.

Emily

A widow of modest means with three grown children, Emily passed away without ever creating a will. As a result, her once-close family was torn apart as the children fought over sentimental possessions.

Tanya

A young woman in her early 20s, she lost both parents within two months of each other. Her mother's denial of her own impending death—and subsequent refusal to originate a will—created an enormous battle between Tanya and her stepbrother, a battle her mother would surely have wanted to avoid.

Lorraine

Her brilliant academic husband, Cooper, could no longer recognize her before he passed away from the effects of heart disease, dementia, and Parkinson's. Knowing Cooper was dying, Lorraine took a proactive approach to the rest of her life. She created a tight professional support network, a filing system, and a workplace in her home for paperwork, and actively engaged her children in the process of preparing for their father's death.

Kristin

Her strong husband, only in his 40s, had a fatal heart attack while at a ski resort with his buddies, leaving her a young widow with two very small boys. Not even close to thinking about how his life would end, Jeff had never set up life insurance or shown Kristin how to handle their family and business finances.

Judy

A financial planner, she thought she had done everything she could to prepare for her husband Bill's death 11 years after a debilitating stroke. Given her professional background, one would expect Judy to have had everything under control, but financial planning doesn't account for family dynamics and the intense emotions that accompany a devastating loss. So, Judy suffered major family upsets after Bill was gone.

Annie

Annie stepped up to the plate to become a loving, competent caregiver for her husband Charles when he began to decline from dementia. But when Annie was given her own terminal diagnosis of colon cancer, the tables were turned. She had to scramble to prepare Charles for life without her.

Sandy

She woke up one morning to find that her husband Harrison, a successful doctor in La Jolla, was no longer breathing. Sandy had to face the enormous, lengthy, complicated sale of his medical practice, and discovered the hard way that not every lawyer and accountant has their clients' best interests in mind.

Patricia

An Army wife who prided herself on being the perfect stay-at-home mom, she was devoted to being a domestic goddess and left the finances to her husband, Jerry. When he surprised her by asking her for a divorce, Patricia was floored … and unprepared. She had no marketable skills outside of the home and no idea how to provide for herself. She was lost.

Susie

She married her high-school sweetheart and lost him to a rare blood disease 36 years later. After spending the last few years of Al's life by his bedside, focused entirely on his well-being and the welfare of their young children, she was both devastated and frustrated when it came time to cope with the practical aftermath of his passing. She had to learn how to use email, fill out financial forms, and track down insurance policies for the first time in her life.

I spoke heart-to-heart with each of these women, and the open and warm conversations were illuminating. These courageous survivors tell stories full of heartbreak and challenges. But to varying degrees, they also tell stories of endurance and adaptation. Their cumulative anecdotes helped me organize this book. Together we'll share tips to help you prepare for the worst (while always expecting the best).

CHAPTER THREE

A Home Is a House Full of Hope—and Surprises

"By failing to prepare, you are preparing to fail."
~ Benjamin Franklin

The white picket fence. The macho man who mowed the lawn, washed the car, barbequed on Sundays, and brought home his paycheck every Friday. The pretty wife who could simultaneously make a casserole and bake tantalizing chocolate-chip cookies while entertaining her three well-behaved, spotless, and perfectly groomed children.

When Larry and I married in 1962, the notion of the perfect union looked something like this. In magazine ads, wives were usually shown wearing kitten heels and frilly aprons, with cigarettes jauntily dangling from their mouths. Men were the breadwinners; women were moms, and they didn't burden themselves with financial or legal matters. As a result, if a man passed away before his wife, what he left behind was not just grief, but often anxiety, depression, and a struggle for survival. This part of the story was never mentioned by the "Mad Men" whose advertising painted a pristine picture of married life.

But Larry and I were a bit more *avant-garde* than the commercials of the time suggested. For starters, we both had jobs. When we married, he was in sales, and I was a teacher. We lived in a chic one-bedroom apartment in a fashionable neighborhood in Brooklyn, and we divided the domestic chores fairly. We would often go to the market together, experiment with gourmet cooking and wine pairing, dream of exotic travel, and entertain friends. We were playing house and having fun with it.

In 1966, Larry and I said goodbye to our family, friends, and careers on the East Coast to create a new, adult life of our own out West. We graduated to a three-bedroom apartment in tony Tiburon, California, and then later to a five-bedroom house up the road in San Rafael. Eventually, we made our big move down to Southern California, to a large home with a pool and acreage so our two daughters could play with their friends, and our golden retriever, Lady, could roam free. There, in Tustin, California, our life continued to grow and change. Larry ran a successful business, and I attempted to take on the role that had been subconsciously embedded in my mind since childhood: the stay-at-home mom.

But I was never the stereotypical '60s mom. We were lucky enough to afford help so I could prioritize quality time with my family over household chores. I was grateful to be able to give my children baths and play games with them, instead of spending all my time on laundry and dishes.

When the kids went off to school, things changed again, and I launched a succession of entrepreneurial careers that made our need for domestic help even greater. Having another adult in the mix gave my children continuity of care when Larry or I had late meetings or needed to travel for work. We had no family in California, so I appreciated the help. It gave us the ability to spend more time with each other and the kids, forging tight bonds and doing the fun stuff.

I was happy and appreciative that I was able to balance a life both outside and inside the home. Sure, there were many uncomfortable moments when the disapproving looks from the other mothers brought up the feelings of guilt I tried hard not to acknowledge. My only two female friends who were not homemakers were doctors. Somehow, in my mind, that was a more forgiving career than business—a man's world. But in spite of hidden censure, or perhaps even hidden envy, I loved my life and felt confident I was a good mother.

The financial aspect of our relationship came easily too. Besides the account that was earmarked for household living, future savings, exotic trips, and cars, we each had individual accounts for spending money, investments, etc. I was a co-signer on Larry's account, and he on mine. Other than my personal spending, though, I left our family finances to Larry. He was excellent at it, loved being in control, and truly embodied the caretaking husband role. Larry was a man's man. He worked with major sports teams and was always surrounded by macho thinkers. For us, as a couple, it worked for Larry to manage the money.

But I never turned a blind eye to our finances. A few decades into our marriage, aware that we needed to be proactive about our eventual passing, we initiated a few important things together:

- Taking out life insurance and other policies
- Creating relationships with an attorney, accountant, and insurance advisor
- Investing wisely
- Committing to never live above our means
- Creating wills and a trust for each other and our kids

I added my two cents about these things and went to all the meetings with Larry. But that's where it ended. Even in the meetings, I really only listened with one ear, knowing Larry would ultimately take care of everything. I was also very involved in my own business back then, and truth be told, I didn't have a lot of time left over to worry about "maybes" and "what ifs," particularly since I trusted his expertise and competency. In my business, International Travel Incentives, I handed all the financial responsibilities, which involved millions of dollars of client revenue. I loved balancing P&L sheets, creating spreadsheets, finding sound investments for my clients, negotiating with suppliers, and drawing up contracts. I felt knowledgeable and capable when it came to financial matters. Still, I didn't get overly involved in our personal family finances. Larry had that covered.

By the '90s, our financial paperwork and tasks had increased, and Larry asked me to take over some of the work. I began to share the responsibility of handling insurance logistics, medical paperwork, and other time-consuming and tedious chores. With my business experience and knack for organization, I knew where all of our important papers were located, and I was anal about creating and filing lists. I had binders filled with information.

When I read these last few paragraphs back to myself, I feel proud and content. It all sounds so good on paper. But what lines up nicely on paper doesn't always translate to a perfect reality. Have you ever ordered a dish from a menu based on a delicious-looking photo or a poetic description, but been disappointed when you saw it on the plate? Such was the case with my crisp, beautiful binders. The papers were all in place, but when I actually needed them, I didn't know what to do with them. They didn't look good to me anymore. In fact, opening that binder was like opening a Pandora's box; the heartache and all the headaches jumped out at me.

If I could do it all over again, I would sit by Larry's side and go over every single piece of paper with a magnifying glass. Even when I began to be more involved in our collective paperwork, there were still plenty of things I left up to Larry. Had I been more involved and proactive, no doubt I would have been able to stay on top of the things that I later discovered had become problematic or even obsolete.

Starting in November 2008, I had to take over where Larry had left off and try to get up to speed quickly on all the legal, financial, and logistical minutiae. We had amassed so much paperwork and so many accounts that it seemed entirely overwhelming. It was an exhausting, lengthy, and complicated project, and while I was going through it, I still had to pay the normal bills and maintain my life in the present. I had to juggle my personal finances and the financial responsibilities Larry had once handled. On top of everything else, I decided to close my business, which involved massive financial and legal work. Then there was the financial and legal settlement with Larry's business partner. Paperwork, questions, and numbers floated around in my head, bumping into each other just as in an arcade game.

I was writing a staggering number of checks and making follow-up phone calls every day. I was proficient in Quicken accounting software through my office, but that wasn't sufficient for my needs. Eventually, I set up QuickBooks to better manage everything, and by establishing electronic funds transfers, I was able to put the checkbook away and start paying bills online. I set up automatic payments for whatever I could. I also organized a new filing system, which further lessoned my daily work. Things fell into place, and I now have a firm grasp on my finances.

But this did not come easy. What I have described in just a few paragraphs took more than a year and a half. Had I been more prepared to begin with, I could have saved myself a lot of grief.

The Traditional Side to a Modern Partnership

In certain ways, my partnership with Larry was pretty modern. But in others, I embodied the traditional role of the wife who stays aloof from family finances. Fortunately, we are well into the 21st century now, and gender roles are getting less and less conservative. Still, if you ask around, I bet you'll find plenty of women who wouldn't know what to do if their husbands were suddenly gone.

When Bria and Michael got married, she was in her early 20s, and he was eight years older. An accountant, he naturally took charge of the couple's bills and finances. In the beginning, this was a pretty simple task. They lived in San Francisco and led a fun, carefree life. Over time, though, things got more complicated. Bria and Michael moved to the suburbs, started making payments on two new cars, and had twins.

Living in the Bay Area is expensive and competitive. Bria held down a stressful job in the advertising industry, working long hours and commuting more than an hour each way. She often had to attend work dinners and after-hours meetings, which made it hard to spend enough time with her kids. When she had any free time, Bria prioritized spending it with family.

Michael's office, on the other hand, was close to the house, and he worked standard 9-to-5 hours. It made sense for Michael to handle the grocery shopping, drive the kids around, and prepare dinner most nights. He also continued to handle their finances, managing all of their insurance, bank accounts, and their budget—which he kept mostly in his head.

Bria and Michael were young and living an idyllic life in a beautiful part of the country. They had two healthy, happy children and lots of friends. They worked hard to make ends meet, and they reaped the rewards with weekends spent at the beach, camping in the redwoods, and skiing at Tahoe. Bria unwound a few times a week with yoga. Michael played golf and basketball and kept in great shape at the gym. They were getting the most out of life.

But the day the twins turned four years old, Michael woke up feeling not quite himself. He had been complaining about pain in his left arm for days. He'd even visited an emergency room a few days earlier, where the pain was misdiagnosed as a pinched nerve in his shoulder. Missing this early sign of a heart attack was an enormous tragedy. Soon after he arrived at work at 9 a.m., Michael collapsed. Within 24 hours, he was dead at age 45.

Bria was in shock. No one had seen this coming. She was only 37 years old—decades away from thinking about planning for either her or Michael's deaths. She felt utterly alone and incredibly distraught, planning her husband's services while surrounded by well-meaning but meddling family members.

Michael's family was Catholic and had very specific thoughts on how his passing should be handled. But Bria and Michael had never been practicing Catholics, and she knew in her heart that he would not want a traditional, heavy Catholic funeral with all its pomp and formality. An accountant in the music industry, most of Michael's friends were a little more "rock and roll" than that.

Because they had not put anything down on paper, Bria had to go head to head with Michael's family in order to plan the service she knew he would have wanted. In the end, she persevered and was able to hold a big memorial service at Michael's favorite golf course, where his industry friends and the musicians he had worked with for years took turns paying Michael homage with speeches straight from the heart—and a little bit of punk rock, too.

Unfortunately, the discord with Michael's family created enormous hostility, with Bria at the center of the storm. No young widow should ever have to endure that sort of stress, all of which could have been easily avoided had this couple made funeral and burial arrangements official in advance. Because of their youth, end-of-life arrangements were never even discussed, and that's common. Bria and Michael were too busy living to think of dying.

A Life Renovation

To make matters worse, once the drama of the funeral was over, Bria realized she had no idea how to handle even the most basic aspects of the couple's finances. She had never paid their bills, didn't know how much they owed on their cars, wasn't sure where Michael had stashed any of their paperwork, and was unclear about their life insurance policies.

With her extremely busy job, she wasn't used to running the household by herself. She had to learn to do all this while grieving the love of her life and helping her 4-year-old twins through the mourning process.

Bria was lucky to have a great network of friends and family around her, who held her up through the immediate aftermath of Michael's death. Her support network stepped in to keep Bria's household humming while she regrouped. She also had a part-time nanny who had known the twins since they were babies, so Maria increased her childcare duties, and Bria took a leave of absence from work. She used this time to get a handle on her new responsibilities at home and to learn how to manage the family finances.

Thankfully, Michael had set up a modest life insurance policy before he died. Bria put most of the payout into savings for future emergencies, but also used a chunk of it to redesign her kitchen. Originally, the kitchen had a wall separating it from the living and dining rooms. It was small and crowded, and made it impossible to keep an eye on her young kids while cooking them meals. So, a designer friend helped her change the layout to a floor plan with a wide-open view of the house. This made it easier for her to cook and clean while keeping an eye on the children when Maria wasn't around.

In fact, Bria reorganized much of her house in order to function as a single parent who would have to multitask more than ever. She created a "home office corner" in the kitchen so she could work from home part of the time and simultaneously keep an eye on the kids. And—a touch I found absolutely lovely—she had giant, poster-sized photographs of her late husband printed on cardstock to hang around the house. She made sure to talk about Michael daily, so her children would have ingrained memories of him as they grew up.

Bria managed to get back on her feet and step into her new role as a single parent. She was young enough to make change fairly swiftly. If anything, Bria's story illustrates for us that age does not matter; pragmatism and preparation is crucial at any age. It's never too early to be ready.

The Bit of Wisdom

Death is the great equalizer. Where once you may have divided up chores and tasks based on personal preference, available time, or skill level, when one partner is gone, the other is forced to be competent in every single area.

What many of us fail to realize is that running a household is like running a business. There are tasks that must be accomplished every day, every week, every month, and every year. And as in a business, things run smoothly if tasks are delegated to various people who are "good at" these particular tasks. This is why domestic partners end up specializing in what they naturally do best, or what works best with their schedules. This might mean one person manages the budget, pays the bills, and takes care of car insurance and maintenance, while another keeps track of the children's schedules, keeps things tidy, and does all the grocery shopping. Sometimes there's crossover, and certain tasks are shared.

On average, women tend to spend an average of 2.2 hours a day on domestic activities such as laundry, cleaning, making dinner, and yard work, while men spend 1.4 hours on these tasks.[3] Together, that's a lot of hours spent on household duties every day. The arrangements are endless. The one commonality in most partnerships, though, is that rarely do both people know how to do *everything*. And that's where the problems begin.

However you divvy up the duties of your partnership—and whatever type of partnership you're in—the takeaway here is to not let yourself get in a position where you're unprepared to handle *all* of the duties inherent in your household. In turn, don't shield your partner from your share of domestic responsibilities. Ultimately, you should both be up to speed on how to do everything.

When I say "everything," I especially mean the things you aren't naturally good at or perhaps interested in. I myself learned this lesson the hard way, and it affected me way more than just emotionally. For me, and the women you'll meet in the next chapter, being even a little bit lackadaisical about family finances had repercussions that resulted in great regret.

―――――⊰⊱―――――

3 "American Time Use Survey," *Bureau of Labor Statistics*, 2014, http://www.bls. gov/TUS/CHARTS/HOUSEHOLD.HTM

CHAPTER FOUR

What You Don't Know CAN Hurt You

"Pragmatism is good prevention for problems."
~ Amit Kalantri

A t any odd hour of almost any day, you could find Larry and me involved in something concerning one of our businesses. Neither of us had a traditional 9-to-5 job; we both had fascinating careers that took us across oceans at various times. We were worldly, and we knew how to play just as hard as we worked. We enjoyed life and were devoted to our children and grandchildren, but we never shirked our professional responsibilities.

The payoff was that we were very happy. We were also financially smart; we accumulated savings, never lived above our means, diversified our investments, and created a comfortable portfolio. But behind that curtain was a complicated estate with many moving parts, and that's where the hidden obstacles lurked.

This is probably a good time to mention that whenever I refer to an *estate* in this book, I'm not necessarily talking about great wealth, mansions, and lifestyles of the rich and famous. *Estate* simply means the compilation of everything you own—which may or may not include one or more homes, cars, bank accounts, investments, and other possessions. Your estate is merely what belongs to you, and we all have one. In our case, the estate included our primary residence, a vacation home, cars, investments, and insurance policies.

The first rude awakening came a few days before Larry passed. As I sat at his bedside in my usual position, listening to his labored breathing and watching the monitor displays rise, fall, and beep, I had a sudden adrenaline rush of concern for the future. I pulled out my laptop and made a spreadsheet of our household budget—my best guess about what we spent every week, month, and year, including the less predictable things like gifts, car repairs, necessary travel expenses, charitable contributions, home maintenance, and other contingencies for the unexpected.

We had never lived from a formal budget before, because we had never had to. But I was already planning to close my business. Due to the economic downturn, the luxury arena in which I worked was no longer thriving. And Larry, of course, would be gone, along with his income. When I saw the cold hard numbers representing the dollars I would require to live without either of our incomes, it seemed impossible. I began to experience fear and overwhelm. Would I have sufficient funds to go on with the life I knew?

In my research since that time, I've learned that almost every widow has the same trepidation. Will she become a bag lady? Will she be forced to sell her belongings? Move in with relatives? Get a second or third job? In most cases, it never comes to these drastic measures, but those dramatic thoughts initially occupy everyone's minds—and that goes for widowers as well.

Larry had always been interested in playing the stock market. He was very good at it—as he was at most everything he pursued—and his wins far surpassed his losses. With this in mind, Larry hadn't believed we needed life insurance. He planned to cover our bases by investing money and taking calculated risks. He did this successfully but never anticipated the devastating recession of 2008. By the time signs of the downturn became clear, he was at the very end of his life, unable to take any action to protect me. Everyone was taking losses, and I turned out to be no exception.

On the other hand, I thought I had planned wisely. I had insisted we have long-term care insurance, against Larry's advice. We paid into it for many years, but in the long run, Larry never used his policy. Looking over the policy today, I pray I never need to live on mine. It's simply not adequate in today's economy.

At the time, we made the most educated and prudent decisions we could about preparing for the end of our lives. I was preemptive about our estate before Larry died, but I didn't go far enough. When he was gone, I found myself crippled by grief and loneliness, while also having to figure out how to handle all of our financial affairs. Our estate was complex, and I wasn't sure where to start. I knew where all the paperwork was but had no idea what steps I needed to take. I did eventually get it all in order, but it became a fulltime job. In the process, I took some big hits—both financially and emotionally.

If you had asked me before Larry died, I would have told you that I was as prepared as I possibly could be. I was proud of my preemptive actions— from a paperwork point of view, anyway. From an emotional perspective, well, that's another story. We are never fully prepared for heartbreak; we can only accept it when it comes. But we must plan for what we *can* control.

Even though I was prepared on paper, in retrospect, I hadn't gone far enough. There were still things I would have done differently (hindsight being 20/20 and all). For instance, had I known then what I know now, I would have:

- Been more proactive with our finances and given more credence to the strong need to protect my family financially. I would have been more involved, learned more, and questioned more.

- Gone over every single piece of paperwork with my husband at least once a year to make sure all details were updated and accurate. It's so simple to overlook this step, which can make all the difference.
- Had a better guideline for exactly what I would need to do in the event of Larry's early death.
- Opened my eyes wide when he became sick and done a better job of balancing positivity with reality.
- Found others I could trust to help me navigate the way without Larry.

From an emotional standpoint, there's one more thing I would have done differently if I had known better: *I would have accepted the person I was in my grieving state* and not listened to others who had different ideas about what I needed to do or feel. Guilt is a powerful enemy, and in the throes of confusion and sadness that accompany being widowed, it's easy to fall prey to its devices.

Almost Is Never Enough

Of all the stories I heard while writing this book, the story of Tracy and Chuck was one of the most intensely surprising to me. You've heard the expression "the shoemaker's children have no shoes"? Tracy and Chuck both worked in finance and banking, and they were quite successful. They certainly knew how to manage their money, because they worked with money every day. In fact, they counseled others on how to prepare for the future, and practiced what they preached for their entire 20-year marriage.

Tracy and Chuck owned their home, managed multiple bank accounts, and had prudent investments. They kept all this information organized in a binder with account numbers and contact people highlighted. They had no children, so they weren't concerned about creating a complicated trust. They didn't think they had missed a thing and felt prepared in case one of them were to die. To simplify matters, just about everything was in both of their names.

And that's your clue to the rest of the story: *"just about everything" is not everything.*

We all remember the banking crisis of 2008 and the ensuing difficult years. Chuck, who had always been successful and confident about his professional life, suddenly found himself floundering in the banking world. He lost one position to the downturn, scrambled to get another one, and then watched as the FDIC took over that bank and left him jobless once again.

Chuck was depressed, and in spite of extensive therapy, it didn't lessen. Like many men, his self-worth was intricately tied to his earning power. No one could know what was going on in Chuck's head and heart, until the rude awakening, when Tracy drove home on one hot, humid evening to find her dream husband hanging from the rafters in their garage. He had committed suicide.

The emotional aftermath of this moment is indescribable. Tracy's grief was staggering, her ability to imagine a future without Chuck nonexistent. It was nearly impossible for her to get out of bed in the morning. To this day, Tracy can't remember the details of that time in her life. "My head was spinning," she told me. "There were words and thoughts swirling around like a violent tornado in my mind." Dealing with the logistics of sorting through their financial paperwork was the last thing she wanted to do, and yet, she had to.

Tracy had her own accounts; Chuck had his. Most were in both their names in case something should happen to either spouse. They pooled their money to pay for everything related to their home and partnership, including living expenses and any domestic items they bought.

Both Tracy and Chuck were entirely capable of managing the bills, but it's usually simpler if one person handles that responsibility, and in this case, Chuck took over, using his personal bank account—one of the only accounts that did not have Tracy's name attached to it.

Suddenly, Tracy had no access to the balance of money in the account used to pay for most of their living expenses. She was forced into a painful and expensive probate process. A year and a half and over $5,000 in legal fees later, she was finally able to access the money in the account. The anguish, effort, and legal details were time-consuming during a period when Tracy was already grieving and struggling to figure out how she would manage. And this was just the tip of the iceberg.

Tracy and Chuck had each taken out expensive life insurance policies to ensure their mortgage payments would always be covered—an excellent idea. But a boilerplate clause in most life insurance policies nullifies them if the policy-holder commits suicide.

Without the funds to cover Chuck's half of the mortgage, Tracy was forced to sell their beautiful home at a great loss. She had to find a new place to live, deal with the enormous hassle of moving all by herself, and then find a way to pay bills on her own. Because Chuck had paid some of their bills out of his personal account, Tracy didn't even know what they owed or when payments were due. She had to wait until past-due notices arrived, then make amends.

Tracy's parents graciously lent her money to cover all her bills while she got back on her feet. She was able to carve out a new—albeit far more modest—life without Chuck. But she still regrets letting Chuck own all the financial responsibility of their partnership.

The message to anyone who is sharing expenses with a spouse is simple: Pay for your lives together from an account with both of your names on it. A simple idea, but often overlooked. Check to make sure you don't end up in the position that Tracy did.

Tracy's sad story does have a happy ending, or at the very least, a new chapter. She eventually found love again with a wonderful friend who was by her side throughout most of her ordeal. Anthony was divorced with three children, and Tracy now has the family she always wanted. But this time, she handles the financial aspects of her relationship more carefully.

Your Unique Estate "Fingerprint"

Think fingerprinting is only for criminals? To the contrary, it was created to protect the innocent from the devious, which is why you have probably been fingerprinted to prove that you're really the person you say you are when signing legal documents, obtaining a driver's license, or proving your identity in a myriad of other situations. Our fingerprints are used to identify us as individuals and for security purposes—an analogy I liken to creating an estate.

You're the only one who has your unique "estate print," and you're the only one who is responsible for it. You must be prepared and knowledgeable, down to where the devil lives: in the details.

This, of course, becomes more complicated if you are married and sharing an estate with someone else. Marriage is a legal contract, and each partner has a fiduciary responsibility to do what's best for the spouse. That includes preparing him or her for the future.

Depending on how complicated your own estate is, you may be dealing with things like:

- Bank accounts
- Insurance policies
- Investment documents
- Assets
- Liabilities
- Legal, governmental, and civil documents

In addition, not every partnership is a traditional man-woman marriage. There are blended families, domestic partnerships, same-sex unions, and all manner of other possibilities. Your own situation will be unique to you, but there is one universal lesson: *The goal of planning for death should always be to save the survivor.*

There is no way to avoid inevitable difficulties, but they can be minimized with proper planning. And you can't just get everything in order once and leave it at that; you have to periodically update things and communicate with your partner about any changes.

The actual laundry list of ways to prepare yourself runs something like this:

- Make sure all accounts are in both of your names.
- Know exactly what insurance policies and investments exist.
- Have an organized system for all your paperwork, and copies that live elsewhere.
- Have a plan for how to liquidate your investments in a time of need.
- Ensure that both partners have access to every single financial aspect of your lives.

Beyond these "to-do items"—which differ from family to family—your overarching goal should be to have a strong handle on the finances, and make sure there are no secrets. Conversations about things like this might not be entirely comfortable, but ultimately they will be *comforting* in the long run. And once you've opened up the conversation about "the end," perhaps that will pave the way for the more intimate conversations you must inevitably have about things like wills, trust, funerals, and burials. As I—and the women I interviewed for this book—can attest, those conversations are never easy, but they are fundamentally important.

CHAPTER FIVE

If You Will It,
It Will Be

"I cannot teach anybody anything.
I can only make them think."

~ *Socrates*

What will happen to that gold watch your father gave you when you graduated from high school? What about your grandmother's crystal collection? That beautiful antique table you found on a balmy spring weekend upstate? The family photo albums?

One of the biggest myths about estate planning is that you only need to do it if you're rich. This could not be further from the truth, and I've seen this mindset get so many people into big trouble. We all have valuables—things that are important to us, either because they cost money, because they have great sentimental value, or for other reasons personal to us alone. A major part of planning your estate is deciding what will happen to all of these things when you die. This is where a will and a trust come in.

Larry was definitely a responsible man, and his family was his top priority. Once we had children, we knew it was time to create a will for each of us. We went to an attorney and took care of the details, which were very simple at the time. We didn't have much, but we wanted our little ones to be protected, no matter what.

In June 1986—almost a quarter century later—we also created a trust. We had no idea what this entailed, so we attended a seminar to learn more. We then met with an attorney, and the rest was easy. Documents were drawn up, and we signed them. We felt very comfortable with this arrangement, although knowing what I now know, we probably should have done it earlier. Luckily we weren't hurt by waiting, but once you have children and assets, a trust is imperative.

At the time, the attorney also had us create healthcare directives and power of attorney designations. These are essential in the event one of the parties becomes incapacitated. These processes were effortless. The papers were signed, notarized, and placed in our safe deposit box.

Change is a fact of life, and so it was that within a few years, we had to go back to our attorney to revise our paperwork. Over time, we made four amendments to our original wills and the trust, including the last one, which occurred after Larry's death.

Making sure all of your trust and estate-related materials are in place might seem like a morbid activity, but it's one of the most important ways to plan for the inevitable.

Nothing Worth Fighting For

If you don't think what you have is worth willing, I'd like to introduce you to Emily, who didn't think so, either. As a result, her children didn't speak to each other for decades after her passing.

A retired millworker whose alcoholic husband had gambled away most of their money, Emily lived on a fixed income in a modest rented home. Even her antiques weren't expensive and wouldn't have fetched much in an estate sale.

Emily's children—Johnny, Elizabeth, and Joe—had always been close. Joe was much younger than his siblings and only a couple years older than Elizabeth's first two sons, who grew up following their uncle around like he was their brother. When Joe eventually had children of his own, they were close in age to Elizabeth's younger kids, and all the cousins were almost like siblings. They played together, walked to school together, roamed the neighborhood together, and had family dinners together several times a week.

When Emily died in 1992, she didn't leave a will or even verbal instructions about how her possessions should be divided up. She assumed the children would figure it out for themselves. Instead, the situation turned into an all-out family feud.

As the baby of the family, Joe had always been his mother's favorite and felt entitled to her possessions. He went to her house the day after the funeral and padlocked the doors to keep his siblings out. Upon realizing this, Elizabeth and Johnny installed their own padlock on top of his to keep their little brother out.

Eventually, Joe got back in and took most everything with him. This included his mother's furniture, jewelry, and even her collection of family photos. Elizabeth and Johnny each ended up with only the few possessions their mother had given them before she died, and their children got a few items Joe hadn't seen fit to take with him. Eddie, for example, managed to salvage a coffee cup he had given his grandmother for her birthday and still displays it proudly on his desk.

Without any legal recourse, Elizabeth and Johnny gave up the fight. But they refused to speak to their little brother for the next 20 years. It wasn't until Johnny was on his deathbed that he asked his younger brother to come for a visit. Elizabeth's first and last conversation with Joe in two decades took place at Johnny's funeral. Joe himself passed away the following year, but Elizabeth still couldn't bring herself to attend his funeral. She hated what had happened to her family, but too much time had passed for those bridges to ever be truly mended.

Elizabeth is gone now, too, but her children still carry the guilt of never again speaking to their once-beloved Uncle Joe. Eddie still remembers seeing Joe in public once or twice, and although he wanted to approach him, he felt like doing so would be a betrayal to his mother. To this day, he regrets not at least saying hi to the man with whom he had made so many fond childhood memories.

Growing Up Fast

When I spoke with Tanya, I was reminded of Emily's story, but Tanya's was even sadder, because she was so young. Only 20 years old, Tanya was attending college out of state when she got the first of two devastating phone calls. Her father had passed away at the very young age of 56. Her parents had been divorced for years, and Tanya was a true daddy's girl. Her father died with no spouse and few possessions and accounts. He left his small estate to her, and his sister took care of sending Tanya the check and telling her how to handle the legalities of the inheritance. Tanya was, of course, devastated, and grateful that the ensuing legal and financial transactions were simple and clean. Little did she know how complicated it could actually be. She would soon find out.

Tanya's mother, Lucy, called her at school one day and asked her to come home. Lucy had been diagnosed with brain cancer and wanted her daughter nearby. Putting those last two courses and her thesis on hold, Tanya flew back immediately.

Thus began a few weeks of intensive, debilitating chemotherapy treatment. Lucy seemed to be doing fairly well under the circumstances, but the cancer had spread. A new, cutting-edge surgery was being performed at a hospital in another state, so Tanya and her mother relocated there for the experimental procedure. Unfortunately, Tanya's mother was not one of the success stories.

Once they returned home, Tanya repeatedly asked Lucy to make a will, but she refused, not wanting to face the reality of her own death. "I'm not dead yet," she would say.

Tanya continued to urge her, telling her that's exactly why she needed to make a will—before it was too late. Perhaps out of denial, a fear of reality, or even the idea that she might give the inevitable an extra push, Lucy never created that will. This huge mistake later caused her daughter much pain and anguish.

There was a 40-year-old stepbrother named Michael in the picture. Tanya and Michael had never had a great relationship. He had been on and off drugs and was not a responsible sort. In speaking with Tanya, I quickly learned that she is an incredibly resourceful, dynamic, strong, efficient, and resilient young lady. Michael was diametrically different.

The family had a small cabin in the northern part of the state, and according to Michael, Lucy had promised it to him. This, however, was never put in writing, and Tanya had a hard time believing her mother would have left her most valuable (and most beloved) piece of property to Michael instead of her.

As Lucy had lain dying, Tanya's stepfather had been so incapacitated by grief that he could hardly get himself out of bed and to work every day. He couldn't bear to see his wife declining and suffering. Michael never came to help, and neither did any of the other relatives. Tanya was alone in taking care of her mother, who needed help on an hourly basis. Ever resourceful, she researched caregivers online and did all the legwork to find the best person to come into their home and help out.

"I wanted to roll up into a ball and die," says Tanya. "But I had no choice. There was no one else to do anything; it was all up to me." When she later had to research hospice options, it was the same story.

When Lucy passed, it was again up to Tanya to make funeral and burial arrangements. She needed a plan of action. After notifying the important people and making the necessary arrangements, Tanya sat alone with a legal pad and pen, brainstorming what she would have to do: call the phone company, cancel credit cards, make arrangements with her mother's bank. The list was long and understandably incomplete, and she did it all by herself. Michael was nowhere in sight, and his father was too devastated to help out. (It's exactly that sort of circumstance that drove me to write *Driving Solo*. There needed to be a one-stop resource for people in this position!)

After all that, the family discord that ensued in the wake of her mother's death, particularly because there was no will, felt especially awful to Tanya. She was bombarded with ugly emotions on top of her existing grief. She relied entirely on her own take-charge personality and used Google once again to find an estate attorney who would be in her corner. After vetting several, she hired one.

Her case was ultimately subject to probate—that expensive, time-consuming, and often easily avoided process. The end result was that Tanya and her stepbrother were ordered to split the house 50/50. Unable to reconcile their problems and share it, they sold it and divided the proceeds. They both lost access to a lovely home with lots of great memories.

Unfortunately, there's even more to this sordid story. There was a small amount owed on Lucy's car, and Tanya was hoping to keep the vehicle by paying it off, but since her name wasn't on the title—and there was no will—the bank intended to repossess it. Back to probate. In this case, Tanya won outright. She was determined to be next of kin, and was allowed to pay off the balance and keep the car, but she couldn't avoid the aggravation (again, preventable) and the constant reminder of what should have been done prior to her mom's death.

Lucy does deserve credit for providing for Tanya in the ways she thought were best: the big picture. She banked locally at a private institution and had a strong relationship with a financial manager who was aware of her wishes to take care of Tanya. He took Tanya under his wing and taught her how to handle many of the logistics in the wake of her mother's death. Today, Tanya gives enormous thanks to this financial advisor for helping her during a very difficult time.

Now 26 years old, Tanya has endured an education far beyond what she learned in school. She was hit hard with "real life" at an early age, and as a result, she's incredibly mature and grounded.

Roll Up Your Sleeves and Dig Deep

A scary 71 percent of adults under 34 do not have a will, and even aging Baby Boomers aren't organized enough in this regard—only 41 percent have drafted theirs.[4] The practical advice I want you to take away from this chapter is that it's a good idea to have a legal will in place, and hopefully a trust as well. It's always a good idea to speak to an accountant and a financial advisor if your estate is complicated, or just for additional reassurance. If you don't yet have such resources, you can always look online for affordable tools that can help. Expand your potential, ask the hard questions, be proactive, and have confidence. If it has to be done (and it does), roll up your sleeves and dig in. Don't be pushed down by others who think you're overreacting or being "morbid." Believe in yourself and always keep learning.

Likewise, 70 percent of American families do not have an estate plan, and this needs to change.[5] An estate plan is not just a will designating who will get what; it may also include such vital information as who will provide for the guardianship of minors or other dependents.

At the very least, a will is mandatory for each person in your partnership, and whether you have a partner or children, a trust is still a good idea. Below you will find some basic information about these very valuable and precautionary documents.

Just as importantly, make sure your beneficiary designations are current.

---

4   Christine Dugas, "Times change wills, yet many Americans don't have one," *USA Today*, April 30, 2012, http://usatoday30.usatoday.com/money/perfi/ basics/story/2012-04-27/preparing-a-will/54632436/1

5   John J. Scroggin, AEP, JD, LL.M., "The Family Love Letter" (booklet), 2012

This is also necessary for any life insurance policies and retirement accounts you might have.

One widow I know lost her husband of many years, only to discover she was not listed as a beneficiary on either of his life insurance policies. One had been set up before they were married and named his father as the beneficiary. For the other policy, he named his sister, hoping to make things "easier" on his wife, who was not adept at handling finances. His assumption was that both of these beneficiaries would pass the money along to his wife upon his death, and they might have. But since both beneficiaries passed away before him, the estate went into probate instead.

A Few Words About Wills and Trusts

Creating a will doesn't have to be an expensive, complicated legal affair. Many community organizations offer pro bono consultations (usually about an hour or so) with qualified attorneys to answer any basic questions you might have. They won't draw up documents or do specific research, but they can be a valuable initial resource. Check with your city's social services department, local senior centers, or retirement villages to learn if these options are available in your area. Geriatric care managers can also provide valuable information if you have concerns about aging relatives, friends, or yourself.

You can also get information about creating wills online. One resource you may want to consider is *LegalZoom.com*. Online resources are not always free, but they are often far less expensive than attorneys. The Red Cross also offers information about creating a will, so you might consider calling 1-800-RED CROSS. Always do your homework, ask around for recommendations, and rely on referrals from people you know and trust.

It's important to note that wills are state specific. For example, a probate proceeding will be required in California if the assets of the estate are worth more than $150,000. This amount in California does not include joint tenancy accounts or accounts with beneficiary designations (retirement plans, generally, and life insurance). Again, be aware that each state has its own governing laws about wills. Don't just take advice from others' experience and stories.

Also note that you can create a valid will without the help of an attorney in some states. Never simply cross out or add information to your documents. In some cases, you may be able to do so in the presence of a notary, but not always. One small error can nullify all of your careful planning for the future.

A trust may help you and your heirs avoid a probate court process, unnecessary income and estate taxes, confusion in the distribution of the assets you've acquired over your lifetime, and even family fallouts. When one person named in a trust dies, there may be provisions for what is known as a Survivors Trust; Exemption Trust; or A, B, or C Trust. An estate lawyer can simplify all of this for you and make sure your family and your estate are protected.

A Few Words About Executors and Trustees

An *executor* and a *trustee* are similar in that they both have a duty of absolute care to the beneficiaries of the estate/trust, but their roles in respect to the beneficiaries are quite different.

The executor, or *executrix*, is responsible for managing the affairs of and settling the estate, including initiating court procedures and filing the deceased's final tax returns.

The trustee acts as the legal owner of trust assets and is responsible for handling any of the assets held in trust, tax filings for the trust, and distributing the assets according to the terms of the trust.

Again, each state has different rules and each situation is unique, so always consult with an attorney or tax advisor.

In most cases, you can designate one person—a family member, friend, or legal representative—as the executor of your estate. If your assets are in a trust, you can designate the trustee and successor trustees, as well. With our aging population, many seniors now find themselves alone, with no one they depend on to handle this responsibility. Bear in mind that if an estate designee is not computer savvy, and not in the position to do extensive research, letter writing, phone-call making, etc., you will be doing them a disservice by appointing them executor or trustee of your estate. Always ask the person if he or she is willing to be in that position, as it does require work.

If you are concerned that the content of your will might provoke fighting among your heirs, rather than appointing a family member as executor, consider engaging the services of an outside professional fiduciary.

A Few Words About Probate

Probate is the legal process by which the estate of a person is administered after his or her death. In some cases, a personal representative may be appointed by the court to distribute the property within the estate according to the Laws of Descent and Distribution. These laws prioritize the order of hereditary succession and may vary from state to state.

If the deceased did not have a trust, his or her estate might be subject to probate, depending on the value of the assets in question and the laws of the state in which he or she lived. (Note that in some states, even if the deceased did have a will, it may be subject to probate depending on the size of the estate and the law of that state.) The process can be very expensive and take years to conclude, as the fine points of probate law are extensive. The details vary from state to state, so it's important to consult with an estate or probate attorney for an overview and advice about the complicated rules where you live. (This is the reason why many Americans are choosing to create a living trust.)

I am not an attorney and can't offer legal advice, but I can give you a general overview of some ways in which people sometimes avoid probate:

- Create a revocable living trust, which will hold your property in trust after your death so that it is not considered part of your probate estate. You appoint a trustee to oversee the trust property, and that trustee can transfer the trust property to your family members, friends, or anyone else you have designated.

- The simplest, safest, and most efficient way to avoid probate with your bank accounts is to have one or more cosigners. Upon your death, the money in your accounts can go directly to the other(s) listed on your account without going through probate.

- **Make sure your property is jointly owned in some way.** When one of the property owners dies, the other one will be given full ownership of the property without having to endure probate. There are several scenarios in which this can occur. Consult with an attorney to learn the details.

- **Gift your property before you die.** If you've already transferred ownership of property, it doesn't have to go through probate. This can be beneficial particularly because the probate process is more expensive as the property in question becomes more valuable. Be aware, however, there are gift-tax ramifications.

- **Prepare to name a beneficiary upon death.** Property with a transfer-on-death beneficiary (TOD) or pay-on-death beneficiary (POD) passes directly to that beneficiary.

I cannot stress this enough: consult with an estate attorney to find out the laws in your state and plan accordingly. Even just creating a simple will—which does not necessarily require legal professional help—is an excellent and highly recommended precaution. *If you don't have anything in writing, you need to do it now!*

CHAPTER SIX

The Party No One Wants to Plan

*"In life prepare for the hard and all you will
encounter will be the required or easy."*

~*Paul Thompson*

At some point, even fleetingly, most of us have imagined what our own passing might be like and what we want to happen. A funeral or a memorial service? A burial or a cremation? An old-fashioned obituary or a simple social media announcement?

While most people have probably entertained this conversation in their minds, many put it out just as quickly. It's natural curiosity to wonder how our lives will be honored after our death, but it's not a pleasant topic to dwell upon. We don't always share our vision with loved ones, never mind setting a plan of action in motion.

In the last chapter, we talked about the vital things you and your loved ones should arrange ahead of time in order to ensure assets are taken care of as the deceased would want—whether they are financially or nostalgically valuable. Wills and trusts impact entire families, so they are indispensable parts of planning for the future. But there is a more intimate step all of us should take when making end-of-life plans: planning for funerals, memorial services, obituaries, and those things that immediately follow loss.

It's never fun, and there's probably never a good time to talk about planning for death, whether it's your own or a loved one's. It's uncomfortable to acknowledge that we won't be here forever. Yet, this book and my message would not be complete, or sincere, if I didn't address this.

Having frank and tender conversations ahead of time will ensure that everything is carried out according to the wishes—and budget—of each individual. Once you're clear about the steps to take, it's easier than you'd imagine. At least, that was my experience.

Because I had lost so many members of my own family, it seemed that when I reached adulthood (or at least thought I had), making plans for my passing was something that had to be done. I remember the exact time in my life when it seemed that I couldn't put it off any longer.

Days before our 40th wedding anniversary, Larry's considerably younger sister, Fran, passed away. She had been sick, but we hadn't realized she was *that* sick. The call came in the middle of the night. Larry was away on a business trip, and my first reaction was to wait until morning to break the news over the phone. I'm glad that thought lasted only a minute, as he deserved to know immediately.

I was a healthy and vibrant 61-year-old; Larry was only three-and-half years older and in incredible shape. The last thing either of us had been thinking about was dying, but the shock of Fran's early death jolted me into action. Funeral and burial plans were the missing link in our preemptive planning. When my time came, I didn't want my children scrambling to determine what I would want. I'd make that part easy for them.

I had to pick an appropriate time to talk to Larry about making plans. My Peter Pan husband didn't want to go anywhere near this subject. I had broached it several times before and never even got to first base with him.

So, I waited until the dust had settled after Fran's death and chose my time wisely to reopen this difficult conversation with Larry: What should happen in the event that either one of us were to die?

Not surprisingly, he didn't want to talk about it. Over almost a half-century together, we had gone to countless funerals. It had reached a point where we each had a designated funeral wardrobe. After a while, we started to wear those outfits too often and hated what they represented for us, so we eventually threw them out. From all these experiences, we did have an agreement that we would follow our religion's tradition when (and if) either of us passed away. That, at least, was something. But it wasn't everything. We also needed to choose a final resting place.

At an early age, I became aware that knowing where I would "end up" was just a part of living. But since it wasn't in my macho husband's plan that either of us would die, he refused to participate in my fixation on securing burial plots. With Fran's death fresh in our minds, I wasn't going to give in again.

Larry agreed that if it was so important to me, it could be another one of "my projects." He wanted nothing to do with it but humored me. I think he knew he'd keep hearing about it if we didn't finally bite the bullet, so he did what it took to quiet me, which suited me just fine.

I made an appointment with a local funeral director with the objective of securing "real estate" in a cemetery. I also wanted to pick out coffins, discuss obituaries, make funeral plans, and all the other necessary and customary logistics. I wanted our children to be spared these horrific tasks when the time came. I was able to do all of this—even write the check—without emotion, because to me, it all seemed quite unreal. It felt like I was planning for an anonymous couple I did not know. It was Jane and John, not Sue and Larry. I took Sue and Larry out of the equation, and this denial tactic worked quite well for me. In fact, I used it often as time went on and Larry eventually became sick.

While I was meeting with the funeral director in our home, Larry drove his car to the beach, put the top down, and tuned in to a Dodger's game. His favorite announcer, Vin Scully, gave the play-by-play as he enjoyed the program and the cool breeze. Larry had no intention of joining the conversation taking place in our aptly named "living" room. Eventually, though, as the sun faded, the dampness set in, and it crept past dinner time, I got a series of phone calls from him: "Is she gone yet?" Much later, I told him it was finally safe to come home. We didn't discuss how I had spent my evening, but I felt calm, knowing everything was in place. Secretly, I'm sure he did, too.

This preparation felt like comforting arms to me many years later when I found myself having to think about burying Larry. My grief at that time was unbearable, and the organizational efforts required of me seemed insurmountable. Not having to make these crucial decisions at that time was a blessing. My plans were seamless and required just a brief meeting with the religious leader and funeral director. I didn't have to face the horror of making those sad decisions in the moment, and for that I am ever grateful to myself.

I also believe that, had I not made the funeral and burial plans ahead of time, I might have gotten swept up in the emotion of the moment and allowed myself to be talked into spending much more money than I really needed to on "upgrades." This is very often the pattern among the bereaved—ask any funeral director. The expenses of a funeral and burial, even in the simplest case, are very high and rising rapidly.

The national median cost of a funeral in 2014 was $7,181, not including the cost of vaults, cemetery plots, grave markers, obituaries, or flowers.[6] And those costs continue to rise year after year. Having made all the decisions with a clear head years in advance, I could simply rest comfortably knowing everything was was taken care of.

Planning for your own funeral when you are young is the way to go, if possible, because at that point it feels like a clinical, paperwork-oriented action, devoid of the reality of your own death. We can still be naïve enough to think death could only happen in the far, far distant future.

---

6   "Trends and Statistics," *National Funeral Directors Association*, 2014, http://nfda.org/about-funeral-service-/trends-and-statistics.html

That's my story. Now let me tell you the story of Lorraine, who handled the passing of her husband in her own way.

Preparing for the Inevitable

He stared at her with a blank expression. He obviously had no idea who she was, and that brought tears to Lorraine's eyes. Her once vibrant, wildly creative husband, Cooper, had been suffering from heart disease, dementia, and Parkinson's for a decade, but his condition had suddenly worsened. Lorraine, his wife of 40 years, could no longer handle his care and knew she would have to place him in a home. It was heartbreaking, and until Cooper's death at 70 ½, she visited him every day.

Required Minimum Distribution

At 70 ½, there is a "Required Minimum Distribution," or RMD: you must start withdrawing from Traditional IRAs, SEP IRAs, SAR-SEP IRAs, SIMPLE IRAs, and 403(b) plans. Note that Roth IRAs do not require withdrawals until after the death of the owner. However, *it's very important to check with your accountant, employer, plan administrator, or other professional to determine the specifics of your particular situation.* Definitely check with your plan sponsor directly if you have any of the following types of accounts: 401(k), profit sharing, money purchase pension, or governmental Section 457 Deferred Compensation Plan. (This information is based on personal research and materials from accountants and other professionals in the tax and pension and retirement fields. I am not a licensed expert, so I urge you to consult your professional advisor.) Bottom line to remember for now: The 70 ½ rule is important to consider when facing loss and the finances that follow.

Cooper had been the dean of a college, passionate about music and theater, and always surrounded by a vast network of friends and colleagues. Lorraine was a kindergarten teacher, adored by her students. They had a nice life, including a beautiful family, monetary comfort, and the wisdom that comes from being lifelong academics. The only thing they were missing, in fact, was Cooper's good health. His diseases just didn't care about his accomplishments.

As Cooper began to decline, he eventually entered hospice care. This was a wake-up call for Lorraine. She knew it was time to prepare for the inevitable. There was little the doctors could do for Cooper anymore, besides try to keep him as comfortable as possible. Lorraine felt she had already mourned for four years, and emotionally, she was prepared. But logistically, she knew it was time to plan for Cooper's inevitable death. Bright and resourceful, she made sure she knew how to pay the bills and run the household.

She also began to contact her team of pros: their attorney, their accountant, their financial advisor. She used these conversations to outline the steps she'd need to take to avoid falling into a financial and legal black hole when Cooper passed. She diligently tackled her to-do list, using the practicality of it to buffer the extreme heartache she was experiencing.

So began her filing system and her tightly organized "home office"—really just a bunch of boxes which she stashed in a room of her house and pulled out to work on every day. Lorraine's dining room table became a staging station for her future. While I don't usually recommend working in these areas (I like to keep them happy, relaxing spots in my own house), Lorraine's wisdom and foresight made it work for her. She made sure to clear the table off every night and put the boxes away, so she could eat dinner without visible reminders of the grief she was about to face.

When Cooper's life support was removed, Lorraine's children were by her side and began to make phone calls to all of the organizations in which Cooper had participated, as well as to friends, support groups, and associates, who in turn were instructed to get the news rolling. Lorraine had organized this sad phone tree in advance, so she didn't have to think about it when the time came.

Despite her intense planning, the paperwork began to roll in almost immediately. There was still so very much to do, and Lorraine's heart was breaking. Luckily, her close-knit family stepped in to quarterback the work. This gave Lorraine additional brainpower to make decisions and take action. She was in charge, but the labor was now divided. Her periods of overwhelm, while still there, were shorter than they might have been. Lorraine's mantra— one I highly admire—was "get help!"

Through it all, Lorraine kept taking care of herself. She exercised, allowed herself a few personal luxuries, and gifted herself *down time* every single day to read books and "check out." She did all this with her head high. There were days when she wanted to dive under the covers and hide, but those days became less and less frequent over time.

Lorraine describes herself as "anal retentive," but her Type A personality wasn't the only motivation for her intense planning. She had also seen Cooper's dad pass away at a relatively young age, leaving a wife who knew nothing about their family finances. Cooper's mom had never written a check, didn't understand the first thing about taxes, knew nothing about home maintenance, and was clueless about handling money matters in general. She was virtually paralyzed after her husband died and relied on her children to take care of her in every way. Lorraine was determined to be a different kind of widow.

But even after all her preparation, Lorraine still had to address the painful problem of Cooper's "things." Even before he passed, she knew he would never again wear his GQ-worthy wardrobe. He had already lost 60 pounds and was unable to function either physically or mentally.

She began to donate items to various charities, clearing out space in the closet so it wouldn't serve as a painful reminder of her husband once he was gone. Perhaps she was a bit overzealous, for when the time came, Lorraine realized she didn't have appropriate attire for Cooper to wear to his own funeral. In fact, she realized all too late that—in her ambitious quest to get organized for "life after Cooper"—she had neglected to think about funeral and burial arrangements at all.

As Cooper's final days approached, the final arrangements seemed too much to bear, especially for someone who thought she had already dotted all the I's and crossed all the T's. Fortunately, a friend gave her the name of a professional who could handle the details, and Lorraine turned over the reins. Being able to lean on a professional made Lorraine's life easier during such a challenging time.

When I asked Lorraine if she would do anything differently, knowing what she now knows, she took some time to mull over my question. Then, she firmly said, "No. It worked out for me, and I'm living a wonderful life today."

The lesson I learned from Lorraine is that even the most prepared face challenges. The goal is to have as few as possible. Sometimes, simply keeping an expert's contact information on hand is the best defense against a lack of preparation. In my work, I have met plenty of people who can help the bereaved in their time of need. I keep their contact information with me at all times, which unfortunately comes in handy—as I'll illustrate in the next story from my own life.

Celebrating Turned to Mourning

Have you ever noticed how many of our memories center around holidays? I'm not talking about wholesome Hallmark memories of generations gathered around the Christmas table, with carolers outside on the snowy porch. Nor do I mean the plethora of red, white, and blue crepe paper on a fun-and-friend-filled Fourth of July. I'm talking about the memories of things we wish *didn't happen* on our birthday, Thanksgiving, or New Year's Eve. You probably have a few of these sorts of memories in your life, and I'm right there with you.

Last Thanksgiving, my only sibling died. As I was packing to fly to New York to help my sister-in-law with my brother's funeral arrangements, I received a call from my daughter. The father of one of her best childhood friends lay dying in the hospital. The end was imminent, and the family didn't know where to turn. They knew I was something of an expert in this subject matter, and I felt I had to step in.

I joined them at the hospital, trying not to mentally relive Larry's hours, when he was also uselessly hooked up to the latest of modern technology, almost unrecognizable. Here was someone else's situation, just like mine, but this time I had answers to the questions: "What do we do next? What about internment? What will this cost? How long will it take? What about informing people? Do we need to arrange for a hearse? Where do we get one? Should we serve food after the funeral? What about flowers? An obituary?" And on and on.

There is a business for every need, and the arena of death is no exception. I gave the family the names and contact information for experts I knew who could help them. I told them to call their clergyman for advice and recommendations. I also suggested they call or visit their local funeral home and a few cemeteries. (Sometimes these two entities are one operation; sometimes they are separate.) The family members divided the work and, after weighing all their options, decided to turn the entire process over to a compassionate and very professional woman who could lift their burden and reduce their stress.

From there, the family's only job was to focus on their loss, their pain, their memories, and each other. As I witnessed their anxiety and overwhelm, I only wished they had planned for the inevitable beforehand. All of this last-minute scrambling could have been avoided had they contacted a planner before the fact. The result would have been the same, only without the angst, the panic, the last-minute franticness, and the increased cost.

I was sorry to miss the memorial event, which nearly 500 people attended to pay their respects. I was already in New York, meeting with my sister-in-law and the funeral director, planning the service and burial for Julian. More *déjà vu*.

Speaking of bad holiday memories, one of my favorite uncles also passed away on Thanksgiving and Larry died just a few weeks before that celebratory day.

Still, Thanksgiving remains my favorite holiday. I'm always with my children and grandchildren and count my blessings. I have so much for which to be grateful, including the warm memories of the people whose lives I lost at that time.

Have the Tough Conversations Now

The most loving way to honor your loved one's legacy is to make sure his or her wishes are carried out after death. The tradition of wearing black to a funeral—as well as intense tear storms and awkward acknowledgments—has been giving way in recent years to celebrations of life rather than maudlin affairs. The latter is likely if preparations aren't secure in advance.

I consider my own funeral planning a success story, but in talking to others, I became painfully aware of how few people adequately plan for their own passing. Only 23 percent of people over the age of 50 have prepaid for even part of their funeral or burial expenses, according to AARP.[7]

It might sound unnerving, but I meet a lot of funeral directors in my line of work. These people have an important, difficult, and sensitive job to do. What they contribute to the conversation is always validation for my message about pre-planning. Those who witness death on a daily basis know from experience that making everything legal and official in advance saves family members from having to go head-to-head about money and other estate matters during a sensitive time.

Funeral directors will also tell you it's a good idea to have conversations

7   Emily Brandon, "Should you prepay your own funeral expenses?," *U.S. News & World Report*, February 15, 2008, http://money.usnews.com/money/retirement/articles/2008/02/15/should-you-prepay-your-own-funeral-expenses

about the "logistics of death" ahead of time—the funeral, the burial, etc. Of all the things I'll suggest to you in this book, I know that this topic might be among the most difficult. But having the courage to face these conversations will help you avoid some of the traps the women I spoke with fell into when their loved ones passed away unexpectedly.

And speaking of tough conversations, in the next chapter we'll tackle what can be one of the hardest for some people: *talking to your spouse about his or her business.*

CHAPTER SEVEN

It's ~~None of~~ All of Your Business

"The greatest enemy of knowledge is not ignorance,
it is the illusion of knowledge."
~ Daniel J. Boorstin

After Larry died, with all the emotional effects and practical logistics I was dealing with, the last thing I thought about was his business. He had been a very successful entrepreneur—as had I—and we had always championed each other professionally. We had great respect for each other's work and often had heart-to-hearts about how to handle work issues, lending each other advice and an alternate perspective. If you had asked me while Larry was alive, I would have said I had greater-than-average knowledge about my husband's professional life. But one can never know everything—or can one?

The last thing I ever expected was to become embroiled in a legal battle with one of Larry's associates, but someone I considered a dear friend came to the table with his own agenda, undoing everything Larry had intended to provide for me through his hard work and entrepreneurship. I was devastated and in total shock. How could this happen? I still don't entirely know the answer to that question.

At the time, I was trying desperately to keep myself together. My grief consumed me; the overwhelming paperwork was drowning me; then this. I suddenly found myself dealing with an attorney, conducting endless meetings, and handling the emotional repercussions of being unintentionally hurt by a close friend. So much disappointment and heartache—not to mention the tedious, time-consuming research, financial impact, and documentation.

My friends and family, too, were upset, watching as my strength and health waned throughout the ordeal. I ended up in the hospital, and that's when I knew that my willfulness to keep my head up and prove I was right was, in fact, wrong. My "friend" and I both maintained (even to this day) that we were right, but we eventually settled the matter. The outcome was extremely unfavorable to me, yet I was glad to have it over. Still, the emotional remnants of the event remain firmly lodged in my heart. The scars are hardly visible, but there is certainly a life lesson there: If there's ever a negotiation, and a peaceful path is unsuccessful, *know when to resign.*

Another important lesson I learned: *Make sure everything is clear and current with your business dealings, and those of your partner.*

Now, I want to share the story of Kristin, a sparkly, effervescent young mom who lost her husband far too soon and learned the same hard lesson about the ramifications of loose ends, both personal and professional.

The Many Headaches of Loss

BFFs. Energetic, smiley, and smart, Kristin—or Ms. Personality, as I often lovingly call her—has been my daughter Dana's "bestie" since they were 12 years old. When they were growing up, Kristin was like another daughter to me, and I relished the times she was around … which seemed like always. To this day, we all adore her.

One day in March 2008, while Larry was in the midst of another grueling chemotherapy session, a call came from Kristin that her 47-year-old husband Jeff had died. Shocked and numbed, we couldn't fathom that he was gone, leaving behind his adoring 41-year-old wife and two little boys, only 4 and 6 years old.

Ironically, just the day before, Kristin and Jeff had attended the funeral of another good friend. Ken, 38 years old, who had leukemia. That very evening, Jeff told Kristin he felt it was a shame that Ken hadn't better prepared for his own death, and he vowed to do better for his own family.

"I would never do that to you" were the very words that reverberated through her head when Kristin received that horrible phone call a day later. He had done the exact thing he had vowed never to do.

Early that morning, Jeff and a friend had driven to a local ski resort for a day away. Out of the blue, he suffered a massive heart attack, and despite the paramedics' efforts in the helicopter, he was gone by the time they arrived at the hospital. No one is really sure what happened, but Jeff had Type I Diabetes, and that probably had something to do with it.

Kristin had to absorb this sudden news while holding her boys very close. Just getting out of bed in the morning and caring for her children was hard enough. She's an extraordinary mom, so through it all, she made certain her children never lacked love, essentials, and the warmth of friends and family. Dealing with the logistics of Jeff's business—well, that was a whole other thing.

Jeff owned his own architectural and building firm, and Kristin had always remained removed from it. That was "Jeff's thing." But now she had to figure out how to pay subcontractors, deal with taxes, and arrange to officially close the business. Adding this to her already overburdened life was a feat, especially when Kristin received a summons to appear in court over one of Jeff's projects. The details of this story I must leave out. Legal encounters are often confidential due to ongoing litigation. These matters often stretch out months or even years—which is just another reason to ensure you and your loved ones try to avoid such confrontational and bitter occurrences.

Luckily for Kristin, one of Jeff's business associates swooped in to save the day. Without his guidance, Kristin would have been lost. Everyone loved Kristin and couldn't bear to see her in pain, so they all pitched in and did their share.

Hiccup After Hiccup

For anyone who has experienced the sort of loss that Kristin did, you might relate to thinking it's all over ... finally, over ... at a certain point. You can stop shuddering when the mail arrives.

And then, surprise, another headache appears.

In Kristin's case, it was a tax dilemma that cropped up much later. Although Jeff died in 2008, tax bills demanding payment on his wages kept coming for years. No matter how often Kristin wrote to the IRS, no matter how many hours she waited on hold and how many buttons she pressed on the phone, the bills and late fees kept coming, year after year. This kind of thing wears survivors down. After an out-of-character, scathing letter to the IRS, she finally received a form letter back declaring the case closed, with no explanation. So far, no more bills have arrived this year.

Another hiccup: Jeff, like many men, had concentrated on providing for his young family financially, but that didn't include life insurance. In addition to having no plan for how to handle the shock of her loss, at the time of Jeff's death, Kristin was scheduled to go back to school as a part-time teacher in the fall. Needless to say, she needed the income more than ever. Social Security would provide for the boys until they turned 18, which helped. But things were tight, to say the least.

On top of everything else, four months before Jeff died, the family had moved into a 3,800-square-foot house that he designed and built. It was located in a beautiful but secluded rural area, and wasn't yet finished, leaving Kristin and the little boys to figure out not only how to live without Jeff, but how to do so in a cavernous, not-quite-built house in the middle of nowhere.

The Most Priceless Gift of All

I can't imagine how Kristin would have handled the news of her husband's death if she didn't have such a strong support network already available to her. Her parents were the first people she called, and because they lived nearby, they were at her house in moments. From the day they got the terrible news, they were there for Kristin and her boys. They were her strength, her rock—always at her side. Jeff came from a large family, and his relatives, too, pitched in to help Kristin in any way they could. Together, these two clans held her up, and she was bolstered even more by her tight community of friends and church members.

Don, Kristin's dad, rolled up his sleeves and acted as quarterback, handling delegation of the details and shielding Kristin from all but the most important phone calls, documentation, and negotiations. Notifications were made, funeral arrangements handled, every detail covered. The only thing Kristin insisted on doing herself was writing the obituary. She was never alone ... except for the grief in her heart.

Kristin was definitely blindsided by losing her young husband so suddenly. Besides a broken heart and immense amounts of fear, she felt angry. Anger is, of course, a natural response to the death of a loved one. Kristin's incredible support network was a lifesaver for her, but she had another important resource and source of strength: her faith, a gift from Jeff.

Jeff had a very strong and devoted attachment to his church and his belief in God. Through his guidance, Kristin and the boys had absorbed this, and the four of them shared an uncrushable faith. When Kristin reflects back on her life with Jeff, she feels sad and wistful, but she also feels profound gratitude for this priceless gift he gave her.

When I first asked Kristin whether she was prepared for her husband's death, she blurted out, "Definitely not!" By the end of our interview, she had completely changed her mind. She told me that Jeff, through his faith, had inadvertently prepared her more than she could ever have done herself. This had allowed her to carry on with life even when the unimaginable happened, to build more strength every day, and to guide her boys with optimism and resolve.

Since Jeff's death, Kristin has been inspired to help other young widows during acute times of turmoil. She has left what was once a pretty cushy comfort zone to inspire and reassure others through speaking to groups—as have I, although I consider Kristin an inspiration to myself and everyone she meets.

Don't Forget to Tie Up Your Camel

When someone passes away, there is more to consider than just getting his or her personal affairs in order. The family is often forced to pick up the pieces of the deceased's business life as well—particularly if he or she was an entrepreneur. Inevitably, someone must step in to tie up loose ends, and that person often ends up being the widow or widower.

As the Arab proverb goes, "Trust in God, but tie your camel." You should always hope for the best, while being prepared for the worst. I'd venture to say that this attitude applies to all parts of our lives, as we'll discover in the next chapter.

CHAPTER EIGHT

The Longer You Wait,
the Harder You Fall

*"Incredible change happens in your life when you
decide to take control of what you do have power over
instead of craving control over what you don't."*

~*Steve Maraboli, author of*
Life, the Truth, and Being Free

It's human nature that if we can possibly avoid something painful, we will. But the bitter irony is that our attempts to avoid discomfort often lead to more pain in the long run.

Under the most trying of circumstances—times when things seem impossible—we have to dig deep and remember that pain sometimes serves a spiritual purpose in our lives. It might be hard to believe, but there can be a positive side to pain.

Think of how you came into this world: From a safe, perfect space in the womb, you emerged into bright overhead lights and the cold air of the hospital surgery room, and were immediately slapped. Perhaps that was your first experience of pain; it certainly was not your last. But from that slap, you quickly learned to start breathing. Roll it forward a few years to when you learned that eating ice cream too fast would give you brain freeze, and that punching your little brother would create conflict with your parents. How about that first big breakup, that poorly thought-through investment, that ill-conceived trip abroad without the proper shots? We learn most important things the hard way, don't we?

Out of many negative situations, we also wake up to the fact that avoidance and inertia can hurt even more than the thing we were trying to avoid or delay. Sometimes, the smartest thing is to face our fears head on. Of course, if the thing you have to face is a terminal illness in yourself or a loved one, this can be easier said than done.

My mother was often ill, but as a teenager I didn't understand the depth of her pain and the limitations it caused her. I never thought of myself as a caregiver; I simply had a sick mother and I had to live around it. She made few demands on me, and her heart issues—starting with a debilitating arrhythmia—didn't interfere with my life, except perhaps that I did more housekeeping than most teenagers.

When I think back to those days, I feel deep pangs of guilt, which I have to shake off by reminding myself that I was very young. I thought the world was simple then and that a coat of makeup, a trip to the hairdresser, and a night out would change any mood or feeling. I never comprehended that her illness was really serious and actually life-threatening. I suppose I naively thought she would live forever. Her sickness was just part of who she was.

My grandmother lived with us during this time, and *her* chronic suffering made sense to me. She was in her 70s, which seemed old to me at the time—although now that I myself am in my 70s, it doesn't seem so old at all. My grandmother never complained and she set a strong example for my mother, who similarly stayed hush about her physical pains. It was only because I went to the doctor with my mother, picked up her numerous prescriptions, and often witnessed days when she couldn't get out of bed that

I knew something wasn't right.

She died when I was 24 years old, after a decade of declining health. While I witnessed her problems escalating, my father died, my grandmother died, and my brother moved away. I eventually became the sole witness to my mother's pain and suffering, a role I did not welcome.

During those difficult years, there were beautiful moments that I will always cherish. When I was 21 years old, my friend Larry and I discovered that our friendship was actually love, and we became engaged. One day, as we were going into the city to run some errands (or so I thought), we stopped for lunch. When we walked into the restaurant, I was stopped in my tracks by the sight of 30 friends and family members sitting around a beautifully decorated table, yelling "SURPRISE!!" It was my bridal shower.

But for such a happy moment in my young life, one memory haunts me: the sight of my mother looking white and lifeless, smiling wanly. I wanted to go over to her and redo her hair, add some color to her pale cheeks and lips, and infuse her with some life. That morning, as I had left the house, the doctor had been at her bedside, trying to stabilize her condition. She was in terrible shape but somehow managed to make it to my shower, despite her chronic suffering. My mother lived for only another three years.

Twenty-four is too young to lose a second parent, and I had no idea how to prepare for it, either emotionally or logistically. When my grandmother, father, aunts, and uncles passed away, my job was to make the telephone calls. I contacted the mortuary, family members, and friends. I was young to have those responsibilities, but I was always a take-charge sort, and death was a natural occurrence in my family. I also made certain the house was in order for guests, there were sufficient refreshments, and clothes were carefully selected for the coffin.

But the important hard work was always in the paper trail that followed. My mother and other family members always handled those tasks. However, when it came time to deal with her passing, and to go through the minute details for the future survival of myself and my brother, it was left up to us.

I can't recall if there was a will. A close relative was an attorney, and he took care of the legal and financial matters. My brother Julian and I handled the rest. We simply divided everything in half. Mom's estate was not complicated. In fact, everything seemed so much simpler in those days.

Could I have been better prepared? Of course, but relatively speaking, I was still just a kid. Luckily, my parents had made it uncomplicated. Also, it was a half century ago. In today's society, no one is ever too young to prepare. There seems to be more affluence and more possibility, not to mention more legal complexity, and therefore more loopholes and juggling with every estate. Our relatively healthy but aging population has created the "sandwich generation"—adults who are taking care of both children and parents at the same time. If you are in that boat, taking care of aging parents, you have a job to do. I didn't know better, but you do.

Facing the Terrible Truth

My mother's death, while not unexpected, was difficult for me at such a young age, but still practically a newlywed, I was vibrant and bounced back. Decades later, when Larry was diagnosed with leukemia, I found myself putting my own health problems aside to focus on him. (I wonder from where I got that character trait?) Like my mother and her mother before her, I grew stoic about my own pain.

Larry's situation was so much more ominous. We thought of his cancer as an acute situation that would be dealt with. He'd be one of the ones to survive the disease, and we'd continue on with our great life together. But as days turned into weeks and then months, every step forward we took resulted in two steps back. His disease became an ongoing presence in our lives together.

We still thought Larry would make it. Even at the end, we were talking about whether we should book a cruise or go sightseeing in an exotic foreign country. Should we spend Thanksgiving with family at home or all go to Hawaii? In retrospect, I wish we had been willing to face reality and prepare for what might happen. Even had Larry lived longer, eventually we would have needed to do some planning.

Denial has often been a word used to describe Larry's attitude about his illness. If you knew Larry like I did, you'd understand that he truly meant to beat leukemia. He knew a few others had and planned to be one of the winners. An excellent writer, he decided to chronicle his journey, so I bought him a beautiful leather-bound book, and on Saturday, July 12, the day of his admission to Hoag Memorial Hospital in Newport Beach, he began the first page of what he titled "A Medical Odyssey." He started by describing the supporting cast—his doctors, nurses, aides—and went on to detail the activities that took place, the gifts he received, and the incredible love he had for me and his entire family. It was a wonderful, poignant, and yes, optimistic account. The last entry, written on January 18, told how the chemotherapy was weakening him, even while doing its job.

From then until the very end, Larry continued to fight back. When he was in remission, and after the bone marrow transplant, he laughed, told jokes, encouraged other patients, and even mentored one. He made everyone around him feel good. That went on until there was no longer any denying that his life was ending. When I told him what was imminent, his words (which will forever be embedded in my mind and heart,) were, **"So, this isn't the end of the chapter. It's the end of the book."**

Best-Laid Plans

When it comes to being prepared, it really doesn't get much better than Judy's story. A successful and extremely intelligent financial planner, Judy was already very familiar with the financial and legal aspects of preparing for death. She also had an 11-year runway to prepare after her husband Bill suffered a debilitating stroke.

In their partnership, Judy had always been the one responsible for finances and for planning just about everything. She knew about their insurance policies, how to correctly name beneficiaries, and what steps to take when the time came. In other words, she knew the "vocabulary" of death.

She'd also had the sad experience of handling things when her parents both passed away in the mid-'90s. As executor of their estates, she'd learned the hard way after following her dad's bad advice: "Just wait for the mail to come and deal with each thing as it arrives." On her second go-round with estate planning, as Bill was dying, she got everything in immaculate order. She had an attorney waiting to take action when needed, documents completely organized, and zero financial surprises waiting in the wings. There were no hidden assets or debts. Judy seemed completely prepared when Bill finally passed away in 1998.

Or so she thought.

At first she was fine. In her sorrow, she even found that focusing on her own post-death to-do list felt oddly comforting. For years, Bill had been on a long and difficult decline, and she hadn't been able to do anything but wait in anguish. Now, amid the chaos of planning the funeral and the emotional blow of her husband's permanent absence, she found comfort in taking care of business. She placed an obituary and planned a memorial service. She called Social Security to arrange for survivor benefits. She contacted the Veteran's Administration to apply for a new military ID and went to the bank to retitle their assets. And she already had a well-funded trust in place to help avoid California's complex and expensive probate process. She was *in control.*

But as the old saying goes: *The best-laid plans of mice and men often go awry.*

There's always a surprise lurking, and Judy's story was no different. The unforeseen issues came in the form of her stepdaughter, Elyse, who came to stay in Judy and Bill's home for the first two weeks after his death, in order to mourn and also to help. But Bill hadn't been clear and open regarding his daughter's inheritance. When Elyse learned Bill had left her less than she expected, she became very angry. And she directed that anger at the survivor: Judy.

Horrible battles ensued, which was almost too much for the already emotionally drained Judy. The climax was that Elyse snuck out early one morning with a suitcase filled with sentimental memorabilia—objects of priceless emotional value to Judy.

Yes, the best laid plans …

The upset with Elyse pushed Judy to make major changes to Bill's original funeral arrangements. He had requested that his body be shipped to Texas so he could be buried near his parents. But as things got more complicated, and she became more and more overwhelmed, Judy decided cremation would be easier. She forewent the Texas plan altogether and instead chose to have a military service near home. This change made good financial sense; she would no longer have to pay to transport his body, buy a plot, or pay for a funeral home in Texas. A veteran's funeral was free, and so was the headstone.

Would Bill mind, she wondered? Was it wrong to go against his wishes? Ultimately, with additional pressure put on her by the battle with Elyse, she felt she had to be practical, not sentimental. "Life is for the living," after all, and Judy had to ease her own burden. The military service went perfectly, and Judy felt a little more in control. The survivor must take care of herself first.

The Comfort of Strangers

Still, two years later, Judy felt herself continuing to struggle with feeling alone and depressed. With the exception of her fallout with Elyse, her friends and family were always by her side. Yet, sometimes she felt like no one truly understood the depth of her heartache from losing Bill.

To compound this loss, she had never been able to recoup those priceless items of nostalgia that represented her 28 years with Bill. Even with a long runway, and all her preparation, losing Bill still made Judy feel alone and empty.

So, two years into her widowhood, Judy decided to go to a spousal support group meeting—a move I know from firsthand experience takes courage and strength. It was there she learned how losing a spouse is like losing a part of your identity—a part of yourself—especially after nearly three decades together. This revelation sounds simple, but for Judy, it was profound. It allowed her to acknowledge the fact she had to rebuild some of her own identity in order to be a whole person again. She started the hard work with the support of that group and has become a stronger person.

She's learned that you become what you do. "For 11 years I made the choice to take care of Bill," she says. "I made the choice to be a loving wife. At the time, it didn't seem like I was making a decision. But now I can see that I was." Since then, she has learned to focus on living her own life in the present, and creating and collecting new mementos.

It has now been seven years since Bill's death, and some days, for Judy, it feels like just yesterday. Every time the homeowner's association accidentally sends her a piece of mail with Bill's name on it, she feels like she has been punched in the gut. And every time she glances at that bookshelf where her photo albums used to be—albums Elyse stole—she mourns the loss of not just her husband, but of her mementos of their life together.

But she is starting to find out who she is on her own, and that is a monumental discovery.

"Plan A didn't really work out, and I'm way past Plan B," laughs Judy. "I'm at least on E or maybe even F at this point." What matters to her now is that she's focused on living the good life and making progress every day.

There Is Only Now

Whether you are sick or close to someone who is dying, it's a consuming, stressful experience to face mortality every single day. You want to maximize your time with your loved ones with every minute you have right now. And doing so is probably the most important item on your to-do list every day.

Still, this is what I know to be true: *The longer you put off preparing for loss, the harder you and your loved ones will fall when it happens.* From my own conversations with people about their lives, I've never seen this proven false. It's the degree of consequence that varies, ranging from sadness to regret to deep depression and even death.

Procrastination might seem like a passive lack of action; but its active effects can be far-reaching. Especially if you are caring for a person in your life who is ill or disabled, or if you yourself are ill or disabled, it's time to start thinking about the future—even if the illness or disability is something you consider chronic, not fatal. You might not want to acknowledge that death can ensue, but the odds could be in that direction. Spend as much time as you can with your loved ones, while you can. You never know when things will change.

At the same time, try to get all your financial, legal, and logistical plans in order. Carve out a little time to figure out how to prioritize your future, and when and how to act on each nuance of the logistics. Get all your family affairs organized, documented, and legally binding. Taking care of all the things that need to be done—both practical and emotional—will be your balm when you really need it.

Of course, every caregiving situation is not about someone dying. Often, the most stressful situations are the ones in which yourself or a loved one is very much alive, but living with a chronic illness or condition that requires constant help and eternal patience. These situations, as I know so well, are no less harrowing and are, in many ways, the hardest things we can endure.

CHAPTER NINE

When You're the Rock—but You Feel Like a Pebble

"It isn't the mountain ahead that wears you out; it's the grain of sand in your shoe."

~ Robert W. Service

Blurred lines—that's how I now describe the role caregiving took in my life. Actually, I never gave the process a name. It was just something I did. Larry was my husband, my best friend, and my soulmate. So, I naturally accepted the role, never considering any other option. My place was by his side, and there's nowhere else I would have rather been.

In the era that it became part of my life, I recall hearing the word *caretaker*. Somewhere along the way, the label changed to *caregiver*, and I realized that I had been living as a modified one for a very long time—long before Larry became ill, long before I even met Larry, for that matter.

At the beginning of this book, I described one of my earliest childhood memories—the day I was sent to my aunt's home because I was too little to attend my grandfather's funeral. Things dramatically changed in my tiny world after that day. We had a large home. My grandparents had the apartment on the ground floor, and my family lived on the second level. Suddenly, my room upstairs was moved, and I shared my grandmother's bedroom. I recall the good parts: She made me breakfast every morning, and it was always topped with steaming, rich hot chocolate. Even today, I still have hot chocolate instead of coffee. I think of it as Proust's *Remembrance of Things Past*.

There were also responsibilities that ensued as my grandmother aged and lost her ability to be totally independent. I was then old enough to help her with shopping, cleaning, cooking, and the task I remember most vividly— and most dreaded—bathing her. A dutiful daughter and granddaughter, I never complained, but I admit I sometimes resented it. Guilt always crept in softly and remained with me.

My mother's illness became more and more apparent around this time. Besides my mother helping my grandmother, my grandmother began helping my mother. I was always somewhere in the middle of this play. My role shifted between the two of them. Wasn't this something all children did?

When I was in my teens, my grandmother died and my father had his first heart attack. It was the precursor to a debilitating stroke that left him with aphasia, damaging parts of the brain responsible for communication. He had complete comprehension but lost some of his speaking and writing skills. He also had lessened mobility, had difficulty walking, and of course, could no longer drive. My attention turned to helping him, which I did with unconditional love. I devoted myself to hours with him, practicing the assignments from the speech therapist, going for walks, reading, and just being together.

This went on for several years. All the while, my mother was getting sicker, and my father was getting weaker, losing weight, and suffering from horrible pain. Once again, I found myself acting as a yo-yo between two sick people I loved. Perhaps because this had become the norm for me and because I had very strong, traditional family bonds, I never questioned my role in the family.

Despite all of this, I had a wonderful childhood. Caregiving was just a part of it. There was an abundance of love and warmth, and laughter always found a way to diffuse the seriousness. I loved school, achieved many awards, had great friends and boyfriends ... and then, Larry. To me, life was good.

There was, however, one other challenge I dealt with over the years. I was a strong and healthy child, but as I grew older, I began to complain about assorted aches and pains that seemingly had no cause. I was constantly going to doctors, always searching for answers but never getting any that satisfied me. I knew my family thought I was a hypochondriac, and I cringed at that thought. I hurt all over, emotionally and physically, and I couldn't cure either type of pain. I could hardly stay awake and never felt like I could function at 100 percent. Still, as a Type A, I did. And it only made me feel worse.

It wasn't until 1988 that I was diagnosed with textbook fibromyalgia—which in those days was a controversial diagnosis without a lot of concrete tests. I've now had this diagnosis for 28 years and have experienced significant ups and downs. During my highs, I've been filled with happiness, gratitude, laughter, a sense of accomplishment, and all the other glorious emotions that go along with living. But the lows, well, you can imagine where they go. Most often, I've been able to fake it through each day, although fibromyalgia is an insidious condition that doesn't present itself with obvious, visible symptoms others can see and understand. Instead, it permeates your every cell, your very sense of being.

After caring for a sick mother for 10 years before she died, and dealing with my fibromyalgia even while witnessing my husband's rapid decline, I am no stranger to the needs of the chronically ill. Still, I was struck by the particular pathos of some of the stories I heard while writing this book. I heard several woeful but heartfelt tales from those who took care of loved ones for a very long time. Some of the women became caregivers for their husbands who were ill; others were charged with hiring and managing outside help. Often each story was a combination of these two scenarios.

In all the stories, I noticed a common thread: Women who become caregivers often lose their own sense of independence and identity—not to mention a lifestyle they once took for granted. It can be a very humbling experience, being the rock. And it's hard to be the rock when you're already feeling so vulnerable and broken down.

This book would not be complete without a chapter on chronic conditions that require caregiving. About 80 percent of older adults have at least one chronic condition, and 50 percent have at least two.[8]

When we talk about "getting prepared," we aren't always talking about losing a loved one. Sometimes, a partner, child, or parent becomes incapacitated, and it lands on us to put their needs before our own. Becoming a caregiver can be a life-altering situation. It often necessitates great shifts in the way we live our lives and handle our budgets and day-to-day schedules—particularly if the one being cared for is the one who used to care for everyone else.

Many of the women I interviewed for this book became caretakers for sick or debilitated partners or parents, for at least a short while.

When the Caregiver Needs a Caregiver

Annie and Charles were married for 56 years before death separated them. They had a beautiful life together, complete with five children, 15 grandchildren, and a marriage that was a partnership in almost every sense of the word. Both worked, both changed diapers, both did housework. Annie was the better cook, but Charles wasn't above whipping up a meal

---

8 "Depression Is Not a Normal Part of Growing Older," *Centers for Disease Control and Prevention*, March 2015, http://www.cdc.gov/aging/mentalhealth/depression.htm

when she didn't have time. The only paternalistic element to their love story involved the financial decision-making. That was Charles's domain, and for many years, Annie was grateful not to have to worry about paying bills or managing the paperwork of their lives.

That is, until Charles suffered a brain bleed that left him with dementia. Unaware this was happening to her strong and seemingly capable husband, Annie didn't step in until it was too late. In his diminished mental state, Charles made several bad financial decisions, which left the couple on the brink of bankruptcy. When they met with an attorney to evaluate whether the situation could be saved, the lawyer asked Annie how much she received each month from Social Security. She was embarrassed to admit she didn't know. Charles had always signed her check and deposited it for her in their joint checking account, along with his own Social Security and pension checks.

Suddenly, Annie had to learn all the inner workings of their finances. She took stock of what they had, created a budget, and learned how to pay bills for the first time in her life. To her credit, she kept the couple out of bankruptcy and even accrued a small savings account.

Over time, Charles's situation worsened until he could no longer drive or do much for himself. Some days he could remember her name and the names of their children and grandchildren; other days he couldn't. Through it all, Annie dutifully took care of him—until she got sick with colon cancer and died a year before he did.

This was not the way it was supposed to happen. Yet, even before her terminal diagnosis, Annie had always worried she would die first. While Charles's mind had been compromised, he was otherwise mostly healthy. She, on the other hand, suffered from heart disease, Type II diabetes, fibromyalgia, anemia, and a host of other chronic health problems. When she had her first quadruple bypass surgery in 1988, the cardiologist told her she would be lucky to live another eight years. Instead, she lived until 2011.

Luckily, Annie had the foresight to take some preemptive action in case her premonition was right. As soon as she got a handle on their finances and legal paperwork, she looped in her granddaughter, Taylor, who shared this story with me. She put Taylor on all bank accounts and life insurance policies, told her which bills would need paying, and filled her in on funeral arrangements that would eventually need to be made for both grandparents.

The plan was that if something happened to Annie, Taylor would manage Charles's life on paper, while Taylor's father would become a full-time, live-in caregiver for his own father. Annie prepared their son for what he would need to do as well: what his father liked to eat for breakfast, how much help he would need in the shower, which medicines he took and when.

When she passed away, her son and granddaughter were able to ensure Charles was well cared for until he died a year later from complications related to his dementia.

Annie had more foresight than many caregivers, who are too focused on their sick loved ones to consider the question: What if something happens to *me*?

The message here for caregivers: *Just because your loved one is sicker than you are doesn't mean you're invincible.*

In my experience talking with other caregivers, I can tell you the stress takes its toll on a person. At one point, while Larry was in City of Hope, I was hospitalized overnight for symptoms born from stress, fear, anxiety, physical exhaustion, and personal neglect. More hospitalizations came after his passing. It never occurred to strong and independent me that anything serious could happen to me while Larry was ill. Rather naïve, I now realize.

The Real Heroes

So rarely do the women who take care of chronically ill, injured, or incapacitated loved ones get the full credit they deserve. The logistics of caregiving can change every facet of life as you know it. You're suddenly spending your days helping someone bathe, eat, dress, get to appointments, and move around in general. You might find your house reconfigured, or even overtaken, by strangers—people you hire to help but who make your house feel a little less like your home.

Amid all of this change and turmoil, it can feel impossible to think ahead. And thinking ahead might seem futile if you have no idea what the future holds. But in this particular situation—perhaps more than any other—you must plan for the possibility of a life alone, and for the possibility of life without you. Are your affairs in order? Is your estate secure? Do you have a Plan B in case something happens to you, the caregiver? And do you know whom to turn to when you have questions about any of the above?

CHAPTER TEN

Grieving, but Not Alone

"Life is not a solo act. It's a huge collaboration."
~ Tim Gunn

Who do you turn to when life gets rough? Who do you confide in when you're struggling and don't have any of the answers? Now, imagine that you are facing the hardest situation you've ever had to face—and the very person you need most is no longer there for you. He's no longer there at all.

There is not a lonelier feeling in the world than losing a loved one. When my husband died, I didn't just feel lonely; I felt utterly alone, unsure where to turn for help with the emotional and practical implications of becoming a widow. I hadn't thought about whom I could ask for help in advance, because I had never considered how important it might be. I was driving solo in every which way, and it was too much for one person to handle.

As many as 25 percent of Americans have no close friends or confidants outside of their family, according to a study published in the *American Sociological Review*.[9] In the last two decades, "Americans' dependence on family as a safety net went up from 57 percent to 80 percent, their dependence on a partner or spouse went up from 5 percent to 9 percent, and fewer friendships has reduced their psychological well-being."

Having a trusted, compassionate person in your corner when you've lost a loved one is equivalent to a life preserver, both literally and figuratively. Yes, we might also be surrounded by myriad friends and family, and that's vital. But there's "the one." In my case, it was my grief counselor, Marilyn Kaplan.

Marilyn's methodology was based on "working through" the grief, which was heart wrenching. I was instructed to spend a prescribed time every day just sitting alone with items of Larry's that were significant to me, holding them and acknowledging that he was gone. I never knew anyone could sob with such intensity. My body would shake, and I would gasp for breath. Marilyn called these "tear storms," and sometimes I wondered whether I could even survive, not only from grief but also my physical reactions during these intense moments.

I wasn't denying my pain; I was giving it credence, and it worked for me. Others told me I was reinforcing my mourning, but I intuitively knew Marilyn's philosophy was right for me. The grief would lessen instead of rearing its head years later, as I've seen happen too many times with others. As Marilyn promised, these storms eventually became less forceful and less frequent.

Marilyn also insisted that I shower and dress every day and eat actual meals, whether they were healthy or not. These tasks are part of most people's natural, everyday routines. But not when you're in "grief world"—another one of Marilyn's coined expressions.

---

9   Miller McPherson, Lynn Smith-Lovin, and Matthew E. Brashears, "Social Isolation in America: Changes in Core Discussion Networks over Two Decades," *American Sociological Review*, June 2006, http://asr.sagepub.com/content/71/3/353

She encouraged me to view myself as my own person, not as part of a couple that relied on Larry's characteristics. After almost a half-century, our beings had intertwined in so many areas that I no longer saw myself as *I* really was. When I reverted to what I thought was my starting point, Marilyn was there to point out the progress I had made. She wouldn't let me drown.

Practical advice came along with the emotional support. I leaned on her, I believed in her, I respected her, and I fought tooth and nail with her, sometimes not wanting to practice the exercises she insisted upon. But I knew she was right. And I attribute climbing out of my abyss to her long-reaching arm, which never tired and never gave up on me.

Marilyn became a pivotal person in my story, and to her I am so grateful. She helped me lift my head up just enough to take care of all of the logistical things I needed to do in the wake of Larry's death. For those things, I was on my own.

The amount of paperwork and phone calls that transpire after a person dies are enormous, and most of the tasks can only be accomplished after the death has actually occurred. There are piles of documents that must be signed and notarized, endless calls and callbacks, and the transfer of assets to be arranged. Even the most prepared person—and I was one of them—can quickly become overwhelmed. I can't imagine what it would have been like if I had not been prepared and had to start from scratch.

This is why, in every talk I give, I stress three crucial things:

1. Form a support network of professionals, friends, and family you can lean on.
2. Ask for and accept their help.
3. Take care of yourself.

The more organized you can be to do the above three things, the better you will fare when the moment comes. You need all three things in place.

Without just one of them, the equation falls apart. In the next chapter, I'll talk more about how crucial it is to take care of yourself, but now, let's focus on the first two items on that list: getting help from a support network.

When I talk about creating a support network, I am really talking about two different groups of people:

1. A team of professionals to help you with the logistics—legal, financial, and otherwise—of death. This team might include an attorney or two, an accountant, a financial advisor, and any number of other professionals who can help you manage your unique situation.

2. A personal support system. We need people around during the good times and people we can vent to and bounce our concerns off when the going gets rough. We certainly need people, perhaps most of all, when we experience great loss. And long after the dust settles.

Almost every woman I spoke with for this book had a story to tell about the subject of support. Assigned to widowhood, most of them realized too late that they didn't have the first clue how to go on. And in almost every case, a combination of personal reserves and outside professional help was the formula that allowed them to survive.

First the Shock, Then the Scramble

Can you imagine waking up one morning to find your spouse cold and not breathing? It happens more often than you think. In fact, it happened to my mother-in-law *twice*—two more times than anyone should have to experience. She didn't speak about it after the first few days. She was a very private woman, so I thought best not to bring it up again.

When I interviewed Sandy, I learned more about this type of horror-movie-like experience. The emotional shock of being a sudden survivor is hard to fathom, and Sandy was forced to put one foot in front of the other in an attempt to forge ahead alone.

Harrison, her husband of 40 years, had been a successful doctor in La Jolla, California. Sandy and Harrison were well off and their estate was complicated, which resulted in a lot of paperwork for Sandy to sort through after Harrison died. She was the organized one who paid the bills and followed the stock market. Harrison—the fun-loving, easygoing one—had been less concerned with his business-related paperwork, and that made it hard for Sandy to find what she needed after he died.

He had kept all his papers in several shoeboxes, which he thought was "good enough," but they were in no particular order. Sandy had to play hide and seek for hours to find anything. Where was the pink slip to the car? The deed to their vacation home? His death wreaked havoc on her, and no one was there to help her out of the quagmire, at least not at first.

Sandy's instinct was to turn to the professionals the couple had always relied upon—their attorney and accountant—but was dismayed to find that neither really had her back in her time of greatest need.

Their attorney hadn't kept his files current, nor were there any contingency plans made for this sort of circumstance. Sandy and Harrison had never initiated a conversation with him about it, and he hadn't gone out of his way to bring up the matter. Even worse, the attorney had made an expensive mistake in their estate paperwork—he failed to record a property the couple had purchased years before—that caused Sandy to have to pay for an expensive probate process. She learned the hard way that not all attorneys are created equal.

As for their longtime accountant, he was away in the wake of Harrison's death and didn't answer Sandy's calls at all. Not ideal.

Choosing the Right People Takes Smarts ... and Guts

Alone, devastated, and unsure where to turn, Sandy was saved by the sudden appearance of an unexpected acquaintance, someone whom she had once helped and who wanted to repay the kindness. This acquaintance helped pick Sandy up off the floor. She rolled up her sleeves, starting making calls, created systems, filled out forms, and became Sandy's lifeline. There are wonderful people in this world.

But there are greedy people, too. After Harrison passed away, one of his old friends stepped forward to pay his respects. He just happened to be an attorney and estate insurance planner. "Wonderful!" thought Sandy. Even more wonderful, he offered to help ease her grief and protect her future by lending his investment skills.

First, he pressured Sandy into making some expensive investments just three months into her widowhood—investments from which he would reap considerable commission rewards. But as she was about to hand over her money to him, there was a sinking feeling in Sandy's gut. She called this man and told him she needed a few more days to think about it, and he lost his temper. He actually yelled at her! He accused her of wasting his time and not being honest. As she shook in disbelief, disappointment, and fear, she thought how Harrison had only been gone 90 days, but his presence seemed so far away. Could this really be her late husband's friend?

Sandy tried to shake it off and even called the man back a few days later to smooth things over. He was curt and ended the conversation abruptly, then disappeared from her life, never to resurface.

Good riddance!

Fortunately, Harrison's office staff was more efficient with important business paperwork, which was useful when Sandy was forced to shut down his medical practice. Even though Sandy worked in the office, she was totally unprepared for the legalities involved in the process of closing a medical practice.

Sandy had to start from scratch. She eventually found a medical colleague of Harrison's who walked her through the lengthy logistics of selling the practice, which brought in far less than she could have gotten had they been properly prepared.

The lesson for Sandy? If she had been more involved in the details of her and Harrison's joint possessions and professional lives from the beginning, she wouldn't have needed to lean on strangers for financial advice. The golden lining is that she has since been able, through trial and error, to assemble a really wonderful network of professionals and friends in her life, including the friend who stepped forward to help her get organized.

Just as important, Sandy has learned to listen to her gut, to surround herself with people who can help lift her up, and to avoid like the plague those who want to bring her down. For that lesson, she is grateful.

Who Is Part of Your Support Network?

Forty million Americans are in the position of caring for their loved ones.[10] In fact, 10 million members of the Millennial generation are already caregivers, and many of them—40 percent—are men, who traditionally aren't as good at establishing a personal network of support.

It might seem illogical to plan a personal support network in advance. Many of the women I interviewed for this book, in fact, told tales of friends and family who spontaneously stepped forward in times of need. But if you look a little closer, you might notice a common thread: people who cultivated relationships with good people all their lives and were also willing to try new experiences at crucial times.

Another commonality I have found: the people who end up with strong, positive support networks around them are the same people who are later willing to *pay it forward*. After all, generosity breeds bounty. I have learned that when we give to others, they pass our strength and knowledge on to others, who in turn pass it on down the line. Our help crosses boundaries and starts an endless chain. We never know how far it reaches or its ultimate worth.

Cultivating deep friendships isn't just a shrewd move for your future; friends actually extend your life. In fact, people who enjoy strong social ties have a 50 percent increased likelihood of survival over people with weak or no social ties, according to a study by researchers from Brigham Young University.[11]

Creating a professional team is a more straightforward endeavor, of

10   "The National Alliance for Caregivers 2015 Report," *AARP Bulletin,* Vol. 56No. 9, November 2015

11   Julianne Holt-Lunstad, Timothy B. Smith, and J. Bradley Layton, "Social Relationships and Mortality Risk: A Meta-analytic Review," *PLos Med,* July 2010, http://journals.plos.org/plosmedicine/article?id=10.1371/journal.pmed.1000316

course. Now is the time to figure out exactly who will be in your corner to help you with the logistics when the time comes. In Part Two of this book, there will be an opportunity for you to make a list (and check it twice). I highly suggest introducing these people to one another in advance, so they can work as a team on your behalf when the time comes that you really need their assistance.

In the meantime, let's talk about the most important thing of all: taking care of yourself and giving yourself permission to live.

CHAPTER ELEVEN

The Fine Art of Reinvention

"An object at rest stays at rest and an object in motion stays in motion."

~ *Newton's Law*

L arry was gone. If I didn't see myself in the mirror, I thought I was gone, too. I don't mean to sound like a drama queen, but this was how I perceived myself. No love, no best friend, no reason to exist. That was 2008. Fast forward to 2016, and I'm every bit alive and thriving. How did this happen? Very gradually. Pain, fear, acceptance, and perseverance have been my path, and that of many others, as well.

At first, there was no relief, only the struggle to put one foot in front of the other, so that's what I did. In reflection, I recall the first activities that took me out of myself after Larry died in November. In December, my daughter arranged to have a large group of friends meet at my house for an early morning walk on the beach to celebrate my birthday. This would be followed by breakfast and permeated with love. I participated. Good for me, but when everyone left, I spent the next few hours crying. I felt a huge void—not to mention sadness, purposelessness, and depression. But, I went on that walk.

Soon after, friends took me to the theatre with great intentions. Unfortunately, the rock musical *Next to Normal* was about loss of love, grief, and resulting insanity. That didn't help. Other friends took me to a movie that turned out to be about a pathetic, lonely, middle-aged single man and woman.

I started to wonder if going out was really the way to healing. But I didn't give up.

I knew I couldn't stay home and vegetate, so when the opportunity presented itself, I begrudgingly went to lunch and dinner with friends— sometimes as the third or fifth wheel, which only reinforced my grief. It's definitely a couple's world. I went to a few charity luncheons, took myself to movies and an auto show, and participated in a current events class and other assorted one-time activities. Deep inside me was the will to live again, but I didn't know how to make it happen.

I thought about starting a new business, going back to school, learning bridge, taking up photography, or doing almost anything that seemed to interest my contemporaries. But none of those things really called to me. When I had the opportunity to be with my young grandchildren, that gave me pleasure, but it wasn't long-lasting. I started going to yoga classes, but as with family time, they had a beginning and an end.

I should probably interject here that my personal definition of happiness is not a constant state of being, but rather a series of fleeting moments that bring contentment and the occasional inexplicable wash of joy. I eventually began to feel and appreciate this sort of thing again. There actually *was* happiness in my life; I just had to open my eyes to it without expectation that it would come in the form of a person.

In my continual search for a direction, I took spiritual and psychological classes at Miraval, a spa in Arizona. I also continued to see my grief therapist. Throughout my periods of misery, I somehow continued to hope for more for my life, and I think that's been my saving grace. I never gave up. With a cavalier attitude, I even tried online dating … briefly.

Something was happening. There was movement. For my 70th birthday I threw myself a very large, elaborate party. Even though Larry was no longer around to shower me with displays of celebration, it didn't mean I wasn't worthy of celebrating myself. This might have been the subconscious turn-around time for me, although the process was so gradual I was hardly aware of it.

I had always loved having people in my home, but entertaining without Larry had little appeal. However, bolstered by the triumph of my birthday party, I began to tentatively host meetings and luncheons in my home— events with purpose. I threw luncheons to thank friends who had helped me recover from shoulder surgery and to honor relatives from out of town. I set up food and beverages, decorated with flowers and candles, and was very conscientious about making my guests feel at home. I started to look for excuses to throw such modest events—anything that would add color, excitement, and liveliness to my home and life. I even invited four couples to dinner one evening. I was making a change and showing progress.

It would have been wonderful and rewarding if my phone was ringing off the hook with people wanting to make plans to get together. That wasn't happening. My friends knew I was keeping very busy and frequently going to my second home in Palm Desert (that's another lonely story), so they waited for me to contact them. It took me a while, but I finally got it. That's what I had to do. I took on the role of arranger, calling people to set up dates to get together. It worked; my calendar was overflowing.

What was actually happening was that I was in the midst of transitioning from my cocoon of grief into butterfly-like action. If survival meant I was to be the one in charge, I was going to take on that role, and I still do. Inertia would be my demise, and I wasn't going to let that happen.

In Search of Purpose

Still, I needed a greater purpose to make my life meaningful again. And I finally found that purpose when I wrote *Driving Solo*. During Larry's illness, there had been literally hundreds of people inquiring about his progress and wanting to send their support. It was impossible to get back to everyone individually, so early on I adopted a practice of writing a generic but detailed email to everyone when I got home from the hospital late at night. I did this for months, until the final email was sent giving the details of the services to honor Larry's passing.

Friends and family would always respond with enthusiasm and encouragement to these emails. Eventually, a few of them suggested I write a book. I dismissed that idea at first. I had never written anything for publication, never even taken a writing class, and didn't think I had the creativity to do anything that "big." What went into writing a book? What about all those pages at the beginning with a myriad of small-print numbers? How do you get published? It seemed out of the question. I also thought of writing as a solitary experience, and the last thing I needed was to be alone with my thoughts, my computer, and my loneliness for hours on end.

I eventually began to realize I had something worthwhile to say. And that message came along with the opportunity to be proactive and determined, two things I'm good at. I've always had a knack for business, and now came the opportunity to create one with real meaning. I had to file legal paperwork to make it "official," set up an office space, figure out how to get materials designed and printed, and build a website. Suddenly, I was learning, I was creating, I was promoting, I was alive. I was … reinventing myself.

I hired an editor and an agent, and made countless calls to promote my endeavor. I soon reaped the results of all the hard work. I began appearing on TV and radio talk shows, was covered by newspapers and magazines, and started speaking pro bono to groups. I donated books to grief groups and then to other organizations, and learned how to sell on Amazon and other outlets.

I now have purpose again. I am determined to keep going with promoting and sharing *Later Is Too Late*. I believe in my message and the truth that one can start life over again. It doesn't happen overnight. It will be different. I admit I loved my old life so much, but I also love my new one. I have wonderful memories—and now I'm actively creating more.

This is what everyone must do after suffering a crucial loss. *We all have a choice: sink to the bottom of the abyss and drown, or learn how to swim again.*

The Perfect Picture Gets Shattered

If *Life Magazine* had written a feature story about the "perfect stay-at-home mom," Patricia would have been on the cover. She was the classic Army wife, married to her sweetheart since the '60s, and felt fortunate to live a great life by his side. As they moved from military base to military base during his years in service, she learned to make friends quickly and always created an amazing network and a rich social life for the couple. Army living also encouraged family values, and within a short period of time, Patricia and Jerry were parents to three wonderful children.

When Jerry eventually left the Army, he ventured into business for himself, and Patricia supported his dream. They scrimped and saved and devised shrewd ways to live economically while he got his business off the ground. Patricia was great at making delicious, nutritious meals on a shoestring budget. She literally and proverbially wore the apron, and she baked, sewed, ironed, read to the children, played games with them, and took them everywhere. Somehow, dinner was always on the table when Jerry got home from work. What a wife!

The only things Patricia did not do were write major checks, pay bills, and manage the family budget. Typical of that era, she left those tasks to Jerry. It never even occurred to her to become involved in their finances.

But as her children grew into teenagers, Patricia and Jerry's idyllic relationship soured, and Jerry eventually asked her for a divorce. While she had known their relationship was crumbling, it never occurred to her that he would leave. Reality hit her hard. She was devastated, depressed, angry, and felt helpless in many ways. How would she handle the boys and support the now-four of them? She'd always had a man take care of her—and a man to take care of. She had no skills, no degree, and no way to bring in money—other than what she received from the settlement, which was meager.

The only thing she had, in fact, was the confidence that she would make it through. She knew how to be frugal, and she went into survival mode. Little by little, Patricia learned to be independent. She proactively took aptitude tests and classes in midlife counseling, and she reached out to everyone she knew for guidance and support. She spoke to lawyers, accountants, entrepreneurs, and teachers—anyone who would listen. She leaned on her church community, and through them, was reminded that she was truly a people person, as she had learned back in her itinerant Army-wife days. She loved to talk and befriend others, and this made her a great networker.

In short, Patricia was an excellent candidate for a profession in real estate. And that's what she did next.

Slowly, Patricia became a strong, independent woman, able to support herself both financially and—this is important—emotionally. She became very savvy in handling contracts, managing money, and making investments.

Eventually, she worked her way to the top of her company.

The death of a spouse is a staggering blow, but it's not the only circumstance that can leave one feeling intensely alone and helpless. Divorce was a crash course in independence for Patricia, and she earned an A+ thanks to the "tutors" she surrounded herself with: her lawyers, accountant, friends, and church community. But although Patricia was able to give this story a happy ending, it didn't turn out to be the end of her troubles at all.

When Life Gives You Lemons ... Again

I wish I could tell you Patricia's resurrection from her marriage was her *happily ever after.* However, it turned out to be just the beginning of another chapter in Patricia's life that once again challenged the former stay-at-home mom to the depth of her soul.

Right around the time I first met Patricia, she had just begun to date again. She was destined to remarry Arnold, a strong man in every way: physically, emotionally, spiritually. He was Mr. Macho, a husband who wanted nothing more than to take great care of his wife, and life was good as they settled into a comfortable routine. They built a house with a view of the ocean, under Arnold's worthy direction. With their two combined families, they had a prodigious household full of grandchildren. They traveled often and spent a great deal of time socializing at church.

After three years together, Arnold retired. Patricia kept working in the real estate industry, motivated not just by the money but by the accolades she received from helping people in her business.

What happened next is unbelievable, shocking, and totally unfair. Patricia and Arnold were at their home at the beach when he went into the ocean for a quick dip ... and didn't come out. He had been caught in the undertow, and, as they so cruelly say, the rest is history. He was rushed by helicopter to the nearest trauma center, put on life support, and given little chance of survival.

But Arnold surprised us all with his great reserves of strength and his can-do attitude. He defied the doctors and survived the ordeal, although he was to spend the rest of his life in a wheelchair, with very limited mobility in his extremities. His mind was still sharp, but he could no longer run the house and manage the finances, and that left Patricia back at square one. She had relinquished those responsibilities when they married eight years before, and had to learn how to do everything from scratch *again*.

With Arnold's disabilities, their cost of living was now astronomical, and Patricia was the one in charge. Once again, she rolled up her sleeves, took a few courses, studied up on financial management, began investing money, paid the bills, and took over all the financial and household tasks Arnold had once managed—all while taking care of Arnold. And she has done a remarkable job.

No one should have to endure the level of tragedy that Patricia has—twice. While she is a strong, vibrant woman who ultimately pulled herself up by her bootstraps and taught herself to be independent and to thrive, the immediate aftermath—first of her divorce, then of her husband's debilitating injury—was rough on her.

What helped her through those moments was her strong community, who rallied to help her create a new life for herself and Arnold. After Arnold's accident, her daughter-in-law, Kelly, helped her manage *everything*. Kelly arranged to have all of the couple's mail sent to her own house so that she could pay their bills, manage their doctor and insurance logistics, and handle any other practicalities that came up.

The couple's friends and church group arranged to have dinner brought to them every single night and to eat with Patricia as she dined. This went on for nine straight months.

Then someone—to this day, Patricia still does not know who—arranged a carpool with drivers to take Arnold to his rehab appointments for the next eight years. People showed up at Patricia and Arnold's doorstep, planned fundraisers to help with Arnold's medical bills, and pitched in, in every conceivable way. Patricia was able to concentrate on the logistics of reconfiguring her home to accommodate her husband's disability, and she employed a live-in caregiver to help out.

With all this support and organization, Patricia feels truly blessed. She decided to give back by opening her home to other quadriplegics and their families. She's hosted events and continues to be involved in supporting the disabled community.

Patricia has once again stepped up to the plate, and once again she has knocked it out of the park. When I asked Patricia what she is most grateful for while weathering this second challenge in her life, she unequivocally said, "My network of friends, my ability to delegate, and probably most importantly, my faith."

From stay-at-home mom to real-estate leader to caregiver who gives back to her entire community, Patricia has certainly proved she is more than just a survivor. Thanks to her faith, her friends, and her relentless drive to care for those she loves, she is also a model of resilience and reinvention.

The Dream Life Unravels

Patricia isn't the only brave and capable woman whose ability to rise from the ashes of tragedy like a phoenix impressed me to the core.

Susie's story starts in a beautiful, love-filled home in Milwaukee. Forty-five years old and living the dream life, Susie was married to her high-school sweetheart, had a new baby, and enjoyed a thriving career as a paralegal. She lived close to a tight-knit extended family and was surrounded by loving friends. From the outside looking in, everything was perfect. Except Susie had just learned her husband Al, 46, had a rare blood disease.

For the next five years, it was in and out of remission for Al, and in and out of fear and angst for Susie. Just as her youngest daughter turned 5 years old, Al's condition worsened, and he began to go in and out of hospitals as well. Their life was a yo-yo of activity and emotions. Eventually, the wear and tear of his treatments forced Al to seek out-of-state medical help, and Susie and her young daughter left their entire lives behind to be with him at a state-of-the-art hospital hundreds of miles from home. They spent his last few months at his bedside, hoping against hope for his recovery. And all this time, Susie tried to provide some semblance of normalcy for her daughter.

Al, a successful entrepreneur and founder of several well-respected companies, had always been very protective of Susie. He admired her intelligence and capability, but at the same time, he tried to shield her from unnecessary burden. As a result, Susie had a good idea of the big picture of their finances but wasn't privy to some of the details.

Oh, how familiar her story sounded to me. I always knew where I could find the details of my financial life with Larry, but I didn't stay mired in the nitty-gritty. I often wonder if it was protective machismo of men of Al and Larry's generation—or perhaps territorial rights—that caused a mental division of labor, separating the major from the minor. So often they left us wives protected, but largely in the dark.

Susie had about a decade to prepare herself for Al's death, but even so, when he was finally gone, she felt completely alone and utterly bewildered about how to handle all the ins and outs of their finances and his estate. Al had prepared her as best he could with a list of the professionals to call, but Susie had never spoken to any of them before Al died, and her initial conversations with them were not as helpful as he had promised.

Oh, how she wished she had taken the time to meet each of these members of her so-called professional support team in advance, to create relationships with them while Al was still alive so he could make introductions and lend his advice. Had she reached out to these people ahead of time, she would not have felt so desperate when she ultimately needed them. As it happened, she had to dig herself out of the trenches of her grief to learn what exemption trusts were, what a Schedule C meant, how to transfer funds, and which credit cards needed to be cancelled. She sat at her desk for hours every day learning how to do all of this while also single-parenting her daughter, returning to work, and running her household.

Susie was only 55 years old when she became a widow, but she had grown up in an era when computers were not a personal extension of ourselves the way they are today. Once our society went digital, she never had to learn new technology, because Al had it covered.

Once he was gone, she had to learn how to use financial forms, email, banking sites, and more. The learning curve was high, and her energy reserves were low. A rude awakening came when she discovered that the insurance company hadn't yet gotten all their records online, so although Al had set up various policies, she could not easily access them and didn't even know how much they were worth.

Here comes the reminder again: *If nothing else, we must be in the know about exactly what policies and accounts we have at our disposal.*

Fortunately for Susie, family members stepped in to help. Her cousin Grace came in from out of state and stayed with her for the first week without Al, holding her hand as they went to the bank, the attorney's office, and the Social Security office. Al's sibling remembered there was more to Al's accounts than Susie had been told. This prompted her to do months and months of frustrating research, which she was ultimately compensated for. (It turned out that one of Al's secretaries had misfiled and misplaced some paperwork—an easy, but disastrous, mistake.)

After Larry died, I had a similar experience. I thought I knew everything about our insurance, but later discovered Larry had a policy through a professional organization he belonged to that even he had forgotten. I came across it by accident and had to hope for the best. Yes, there was a claim, which was complicated to file, but still a nice surprise. Another surprise was to discover that the value diminished with age, and since Larry was 71 years old when he died, the payoff was insignificant. (So much for the golden years.)

Today, Susie has an assistant who helps her keep her papers in order and teaches her computer literacy and financial skills. Susie doesn't just outsource the work; she sits side by side with her assistant and requests an explanation for every little thing. She wants to know exactly how to handle all aspects of her financial life. This ultimately makes her feel in control and capable.

When Susie married Al, she never planned to live without him—not at such a young age anyway. But anything can happen, and when Al passed away, she proved to be a resilient and resourceful woman. Her willingness to face her future and learn how to reinvent herself is the single reason she is thriving today.

Find Yourself Again

For Patricia, and Susie, and me, it wasn't (and still isn't) easy all the time. Even now, I have to remind myself to have a light attitude when it comes to the many new experiences I have as a single woman. Last June, for instance, I decided I needed to get my Hawaii fix but had no one with whom to go. So, I went by myself. I'm very friendly and sociable and instinctively felt I'd meet people there.

Guess what? One week later, and the only people with whom I'd had conversations were the wait staff, bellmen, and drivers. Yet, I smiled to myself the whole time. Was I sad or depressed? No. Was I lonely? Yes!

But, I had a wonderful time. I got dressed every night and had a beautiful dinner at my table for one. I was participating in life, even though it wasn't how I had envisioned my life would be, and I was proud I could still laugh and enjoy myself.

As I've learned again and again throughout my life, *a good sense of humor can be your saving grace, even when life doesn't seem the least bit funny.*

CHAPTER TWELVE

What Matters in the End

"Life isn't about finding yourself.
Life is about creating yourself."
~ George Bernard Shaw

Did you know there were once Four Stooges? I only know this because my favorite uncle, Jimmy Brewster, was actually the fourth Stooge—until they became the famous *Three* Stooges. He was a comic force in Hollywood, performing in nightclubs and occasionally landing a movie role.

In fact, I come from a long line of comedians, both amateur and professional. So it is no surprise that laughter had a huge presence in my family. I was always surrounded by storytellers and jokesters, imbuing my childhood with a playful sense of camaraderie and a "show must go on!" bravado. When I think about my family, I think of classic Shakespearean plays, where a character is often weaved into dramatic storylines just to provide comic relief. That person would have been a relative of mine.

In my immediate family, my mother was always the joke teller. She liked to perform in amateur productions during our summer vacations. One summer she even performed a routine with Danny Kaye!

One of my favorite stories about my mom was set in a hospital room. She was hooked up to machines, surrounded by retro-1960s tubes and computers. Yet, she was still very much herself: lucid and funny. My best friend, Myrna—in her early 20s, breathtakingly gorgeous, and single—came to visit. Suddenly, my mother feigned a need for a doctor—STAT!—and an extremely handsome, young, single doctor (whom Mother knew was on duty) waltzed in. Do I need to finish?

Yes, my mother felt "suddenly better" when he arrived. She introduced him to Myrna, made herself comfortable, closed her eyes, and let them talk and form some sort of common bond. Who knew where it would lead?

That tricky behavior was pretty typical for my mother. When the hunky doctor left, she and Myrna were in hysterics. Oh, how I wish I had been there!

In terms of entertainment ability, my aunt was a close second to my mother. She looked like a cross between Myrna Loy and Lucille Ball, and she could make people laugh just as hard as Lucy. My brother was dry, sharp, and quick-witted. And I, of course, married a funny man. Larry was the ever-playful master of ceremonies, quick to crack jokes of any kind, depending upon his audience. He would have people thinking and laughing for hours.

We passed this love of laughter on to our children, Dana and Bari, who, in turn, have passed it on to theirs. Despite the sad subject matter I've made into a career, I've been told I have a pretty good sense of humor myself. When my family gets together, the room is filled with laughter, self-deprecation, and compassionate sarcasm. This, despite all the losses we have faced together.

I'm probably not the first person to tell you that having a sense of humor is imperative in times of stress. Studies have long shown that a good bout of laughter can relieve stress, boost the immune system, and reduce the risk of heart attack and stroke.

On a personal note, I recall several times when I was in mourning for relatives, and friends came to the house to pay their respects with the expectation of finding a somber, morbid environment, only to be met with laughter and fond reminiscing. This definitely confused those outside our world, but they left feeling good and comfortable. Like Canio in the opera *Pagliacci*, we knew how to laugh on the outside while crying on the inside.

Why bring this up now?

Death of a spouse is considered the number one stressor in life, according to the Holmes-Rahe Stress Scale.[12] And widowhood increases a person's risk of dying.[13] After all the financial details are sorted out, the wills drawn up, the memorial plans secured, and the household organized, there is still one very important thing left to attend to: YOU.

I consider self-care to be the most important element to survival. And it starts right now—not after a loved one has passed away, but *now*, with your sense of humor, your ability to take care of yourself, and your willingness to go on.

Secure Your Own Oxygen Mask First

Before Larry's diagnosis, I always exercised. I swam, walked, played tennis, and worked out with a trainer. I was also very nutrition-conscious, especially because I had a family history of early deaths from heart disease and strokes. You better believe I wasn't going to give in to the odds without doing everything I could to protect myself! Whatever the latest medical news said, I was on it, switching to this or that healthy eating plan. First, I cut out this food. Then, I added it back in and cut out the next one. I had massages, went to spas, meditated. In short, I did all the right things.

After Larry's death, I did very little. In fact, even my eating was limited

---

13   Felix Elwert, Ph.D., and Nicholas A. Christakis, MD, Ph.D., MPH, "The Effect of Widowhood on Mortality by the Causes of Death of Both Spouses," *US National Library of Medicine, National Institutes of Health*, November 2008, http://www.ncbi.nlm.nih.gov/pmc/articles/PMC2636447/

because preparing meals for myself seemed absurd. I lost weight and looked frail. I walked with some regularity, but that was it. Forget the spas, the massages, the meditation. Forget the time for myself. I did not follow the advice that I now give everyone, and the results were disastrous.

Please consider me proof that self-care should always be your number one priority. Grief can be cruel. We mourn the dead and treat ourselves with little respect. It's as if we're dead, too. It's as if we don't count.

But we do.

So far, this entire book has been about getting prepared for what may come, and in Part Two, I'll guide you on how to take active control of your unique situation and future. But before we go there, let's take a moment to talk about *right now*.

Of all the things that I advocate women do to prepare for the future, by far the most important is to learn how to take care of yourself. I mean really take care of yourself ... put YOU first. For many women, this means learning how to eat right, getting enough sleep, and making time for a little exercise every day. For others, it means learning how to back off the pressure and expectations we put on ourselves to be perfect—perfect daughters, perfect wives, perfect mothers, perfect grandmothers—and how to simply say "no."

Maybe you already know how you could take better care of yourself, but you're not doing it. I urge you to do it now. Because when the worst happens, that disposition toward self-care will be the most valuable weapon in your arsenal.

The "Now" Bucket List

Unlike a regular bucket list, this one is not about all the grand things you want to accomplish before you die. It's about the little things you wish you were doing *right now*. The things you crave, the passions that ignite you but that you put off in lieu of finishing your daily to-do list.

Write down five things you would rather be doing than working on the directives in this book. Things like "take an art class," "learn French," "visit my college roommate on the other side of the country," "attend a local football game."

1. _____

2. _____

3. _____

4. _____

5. _____

Now, do these things—or at least one of them. Go ahead, give yourself permission! The paperwork can wait; the phone calls can wait; all the stress can wait. Take yourself on a date. Rediscover what it means to live for this very moment, to do something for yourself for a change.

Then it's time to get to work.

Lessons Learned
the Not-So-Hard Way

We all experience loss, and we must all learn to go on. My hope for you is that you won't experience great loss in your life at all. But that's not realistic. When it happens, you will feel like you will never truly enjoy life again. You will feel broken, maybe even unwilling to go on. But you *will* go on. You might even flourish. You might learn from your darkest experiences and emerge like a phoenix—a stronger, more powerful person. This is what happened for me. And it is what I want for you, too.

One day, you might need to go on with your life without your loved one by your side. Having the conviction to do that, knowing what to do, and believing *you can do it* will save your life.

There's an old saying that a fool learns from his own mistakes, but a wise man learns from the mistakes of others. Throughout the writing of this book, the women I interviewed embodied the knowledge they had to learn firsthand, without the benefit of learning from others, and I congratulate them. They did the best they could with the cards they were given. But we all have one thing in common: We share our stories in the hopes that others can learn from our mistakes or naiveties, and perhaps not suffer as much when they find themselves in the same situation.

As I interviewed the women whose stories fill this book, I was struck by how each and every one of them was thrown into a situation they would never have chosen and emerged victorious, survivors. For some, it was a long, painful process. Others had the genetic makeup and the planning skills to shorten the lifecycle of grief and mourning. But ultimately, they all figured out how to take care of themselves, and each had a valuable lesson to teach.

Bria taught us the value of having an organized domestic situation in case one is ever in the position of single parenting. Tracy taught us to mind the details when it comes to finances—especially if you share them with another person— and to have an airtight plan for your estate, no matter what (or how little) it consists of. Elizabeth taught us that even a small estate could create problems if it's not planned correctly, and Tanya's story reiterated the importance of having a legal will in place.

Lorraine, a shining example of a person who was as prepared as possible, showed us how even the most organized survivors should be ready to hit snags. Kristin illustrated how vital it is to have a handle on your partner's professional life. Judy's story taught us about setting inheritance expectations with one's loved ones, and Annie showed us why caregivers can't take their own health for granted. Sandy illuminated how important it is to have the right support networks in place—both personal and professional. And both Patricia and Sandy taught us that resilience starts with the willingness to learn new things.

As for me, I continue to teach myself—and let the universe teach me— lessons all the time. I'm sure I will never stop learning. At least, I hope not!

We all have to be proactive. You're the one who will have to make it happen, whatever "it" is for you. And when it comes to self-care, I've found, resilience is directly related to one's ability to laugh at oneself and at life.

Now, get ready to put these life lessons into action in Part Two.

PART TWO

Part Two Table of Contents

Control Without Chaos..151

A Quick Note About "Who"..153

Getting Started 155

    Create a Workspace..156

    Get Organized..157

    Share Your Work..159

    The Only Constant Is Change................................160

Worksheets and Checklists..161

Fast Facts for Reference...163

Financial...164

    Financial Contacts...165

    Assets...167

    Insurance & Other Policies....................................181

    Liabilities...202

Legal & Estate..213

Business...218

Personal and Domestic Information..241

Caregiving..248

End-of-Life Arrangements...250

When the Time Comes, What to Do First...............................257

First Hours and Days...258

First-Priority Tasks...259

Second-Priority Tasks...260

Third-Priority Tasks...261

Control Without Chaos

"Facts do not cease to exist because they are ignored."

~ Aldous Huxley

Congratulations! By having the courage to tackle the checklists and worksheets in this section, you are actually challenging the Chaos to Control program I developed for recent widows and widowers. Instead, you are going straight to control, thereby preventing the chaos from ever happening.

I am, therefore, very happy to rename your work "Control Without Chaos." This is my intention and the reason for the years of research to which I've devoted myself, so that you can have an easier time when facing loss. Thank you for your trust in me.

Now that you're actually here in Part Two, I hope you're feeling motivated to begin this most important project. Slowly, one step at a time (as the Chinese proverb so aptly states), is how the thousand-mile journey begins. It might seem daunting, but the rewards will be worth it. You will feel liberated when you are done, and when the information you are about to gather is finally needed, you will have given yourself and your family the freedom to handle adversity with less stress, anxiety, and costly errors. Kudos to you for starting.

As you tackle Part Two, keep in mind that this book was designed for *everyone*. You are not everyone; *you are you*. This is a guide—a substantial overview—and for many people, it will serve as a comprehensive document that covers every detail. For some, it will be too in-depth, and I encourage you to fill out only the worksheets that apply to you and ignore the rest. Others may find they need more worksheets to properly capture all of their information. *For this reason, I have included blank pages at the back of the worksheets section, and you can also find duplicate worksheets on my website at* http://susanalpertconsulting.com/downloads.

No matter your particular situation, as you work through Part Two, keep in mind that it is not a "one-size-fits-all" instruction manual. But it *is* a great working document, with a friendly and easy format—that will work just for you.

I have tried to be very specific in what you need to do to prepare, so you won't feel lost—now or later—and you won't miss a thing. As you read, focus on the pages and sections that are applicable to you. Remember to be flexible, and (this is very important!) make sure you are pausing to put the book down and take deep breaths once in a while.

Let's dive in.

A Quick Note About "Who"

"Planning is bringing the future into the present so that you can do something about it now."

~ *Alan Lakein*

Are you planning ahead for yourself? Your spouse? A parent? Another loved one? Or perhaps for the couple of whom you are half, with joint assets and responsibilities? I suggest first getting clear on "who" this is all about, so that when you start to fill out the worksheets and get your paperwork in order, you know exactly what you need.

Remember to stay on track and focused. This process is designed for going at your own pace. The last thing you want to do is create a stressful and overwhelming task for yourself. After all, isn't that why you are reading this book—to avoid getting overwhelmed at all?

On the other hand, try to keep the momentum going. If you step away from the project for too long, you risk giving up on it altogether. Remember, *slow and steady.*

Getting Started

*"Divide your movements into easy-
to-do sections. If you fail, divide again."*

~ Peter Nivio Zarlenga

Later Is Too Late is about prevention and vigilance. It's about taking care of yourself first. We all want to be prepared, but many of us don't know what steps to take. I'll take those first steps with you, right now, in a very purposeful and concrete way. Throughout the process of Part Two, we'll address preparedness, readiness, and attention to detail.

There is a lot of work to be done, but the good news is that you can navigate through these tasks, checklists, and worksheets at a pace that doesn't feel overwhelming. I suggest putting aside an hour or two a week until all of the tasks at hand are completed.

As a quick overview, here's what you'll be documenting along the way:

- **Financial matters:** information for various types of personal insurance, bank accounts, investments, and retirement accounts, as well as contact information for accountants, financial advisors, insurance brokers, and others

- **Legal matters:** wills, trusts, guardianship directives, powers of attorney, and information about your estate, including collectables

- **Business details:** business insurance, computer and filing information, contact lists for professional associates

- **Personal and domestic matters:** personal IDs, medical records, household service contacts and manuals

- **Caregiving:** information and instructions regarding others in your life for whom you may be responsible

- **End-of-life plans:** funeral and burial arrangements, organ donation information

At each step, I'll explain exactly what information you need to write down and file. Your goal will be to organize, document, and in some cases, simplify the accounts, policies, and other important components of both your life and your estate.

Create a Workspace

Before getting started, let's talk about where you will work. Do you have a home office? A desk tucked away in a nook right next to a filing cabinet? If so, you are lucky. This "business area" of your house is the perfect place to set up camp while working on this project.

If you don't have a designated home office space, you'll have to decide where the most convenient place will be to spread out your paperwork and begin to get organized. I recommend that you don't work at the kitchen table, on the bed, or in front of the TV. Ideally, you want to keep this project separate from the places you live in and enjoy on a daily basis. Those spaces are part of your living present. Let's keep them that way.

You won't need much for this project besides yourself, this book, and a willingness to be proactive. But a few things that might come in handy include:

- Your contact list—whether it's on your phone or computer, written down in an address book, or in a rolodex filled with business cards

- Copies of important bills, account information, statements, contracts, and documents

- The mail: This is one of your most important resources for information. Each day, scour the mail for letters from credit card companies, insurance providers, and other professionals (attorneys, accountants, financial advisors). This will help you fill in the blanks in this book with current, concrete information.

Get Organized

Where do you lie on the organization spectrum? Are you fastidious and compulsive about filing your important paperwork—with alphabetized, multicolored folders and labeled file cabinets? Or are you more of a "throw it in that pile; I'll get to it later" type of person? The first step to getting organized is coming to terms with your own organizational style. Everyone has a style that works for them—although admittedly, some styles are more efficient than others.

If you have a system that works well for you, by all means, stick to it. But if you're looking for some direction, here's what I suggest. First, you'll need file folders of two types:

1. Regular manila folders

2. Larger folders you can nest several manila folders in—either hanging file folders or accordion folders

The larger folders will serve as "master" folders for the main topic. Then you can place manila folders—the "subfolders"—in each master folder for your various accounts. For instance, you might have a master "insurance" folder with several subfolders for health insurance, car insurance, life insurance, etc.

Just as important as having organized folders is having them properly labeled. Don't forget to label every single file and folder in a way that works for you: handwritten, printed stickers, etc. I invested in a handheld label maker (anywhere from $15 to $30 and one of my favorite gadgets).

To get started, label the "master" folders with broad categories, such as those we'll cover in this book. Again, those include:

- Financial
- Legal
- Business
- Personal/domestic
- Caregiving
- End-of-life plans

Many of us techies prefer to do as much filing and organizing on our computers as possible, which is one reason I provide digital versions of the following worksheets on my website at http://susanalpertconsulting.com/ downloads. However, you will always have some critical information on paper, such as signed agreements and important pieces of mail. You'll need some sort of paper filing system.

Share Your Work

A crucial element to this project I want to mention early on, before we get started with the nitty gritty, is to share the information with someone else. If you have a partner, it's vital that he or she knows the whereabouts of your sensitive information. If you're keeping it on your computer, share the password and explain where to find documents and folders. The same goes for your paper filing system.

I also urge you to let at least one, if not all, of your adult children or heirs know that you are doing this work and where to find the relevant paperwork when the time comes. As a safety precaution, it's also a good idea to create copies of important papers and send them to at least one person in your life whom you trust. Otherwise, if there were ever a flood or fire at your home, you risk losing the only copies you have.

This piece of advice might raise the "privacy red flag" for you, but if you're nervous about sharing private data now, consider investing in a safe deposit box. Just make sure at least one other person has access to it when the time comes. If you're less concerned with privacy and security issues, you could seal the copies of your documents in a large envelope and ask the recipient not to open it until something happens to you.

The Only Constant Is Change

Over the next few weeks, you'll create a comprehensive system of organized information that will serve as a repository for everything you—or your loved ones—will need to access when the time comes. But the project doesn't end there. Hopefully, it will be years, even decades, before you need this information. During that time, certain things will change—your insurance policies might shift; your will might need updating; your various and many different types of accounts will require updated information. Some will be cancelled; you might acquire some new ones.

It's important to keep all of this information up to date, so I suggest scheduling a time once or twice a year to review all documents and update anything that has changed. If you use a calendar—either on your computer or on paper—set yourself an appointment in the future, and make it a recurring appointment.

If you have a partner, make certain you're both involved with the updates. Everyone is so busy, and your partner may have information he or she has neglected to share with you, and vice versa. You may also choose to involve adult children or other close loved ones in the process. You'll have to find your own balance between prudent sharing and maintaining a comfortable element of privacy.

Another important part of keeping your information updated—one that so many people overlook, to disastrous results later on—is to share the changes with whichever loved ones or professionals you've chosen to be the "keeper" of your copies. If you've told someone in your life where to find your vital information when the time comes, an annual reminder is a great idea, too.

I encourage you to write all of this information down in pencil or have whiteout handy to make changes in the future.

Worksheets and Checklists

"A good plan is like a road map: it shows the final
destination and usually the best way to get there."

~ *H. Stanley Judd*

Sure, you have most or all of the information I'm going to ask you to fill out already written down, here and there. You have insurance cards, monthly bills, and all sorts of other paperwork ... somewhere. The question is, where? Is it all neatly filed in one place? Do you keep it updated? If someone needed to access all your important account numbers and crucial pieces of data, would they even know where to look or whom to ask?

The purpose of the worksheets that follow this page are to help you get all of your vital information gathered and organized in one easy place—a "one-stop shop" for your data. Remember those folders you created? These worksheets and checklists follow the same organizational scheme I recommended for the folders:

- Financial
- Legal

- Business
- Personal/domestic
- Caregiving
- End-of-life plans

Each category begins with a page or two for "At a Glance" information —items you want to have easy access to when you need it. The "At a Glance" pages will serve as a complete list of your contacts, assets, liabilities, and other types of information within each category. I suggest bookmarking the "At a Glance" pages.

Following these pages, the next section has detailed worksheets so you can include all other relevant content.

As you go through this section, remember that not every worksheet will apply to you. You may not have life insurance, for instance, or a financial advisor, or more than one vehicle. Fill out what is relevant to your particular situation. Ignore the rest.

On the other hand, you may have three types of life insurance and need more worksheets than are provided in this book. If so, there are empty pages at the back of this section for writing down additional information. *Or go to my website at* http://susanalpertconsulting.com/downloads **to download extra copies of all of these worksheets.**

My hope is that this list of worksheets will also help you fill in the blanks on what you're missing in the big picture of your life. Perhaps you've always meant to get life insurance but haven't gotten around to it yet. Maybe a will is something you've thought about but haven't created or had notarized. Now is the time. As you go through these exercises, take note of where you need to do more work. Then ACT. This is a perfect time to take action. *Later is too late.*

Fast Facts for Reference

Full name _____

Place of birth _____

Date of birth _____

Mother's maiden name _____

Social Security number _____

Blood Type _____

Current address _____

_____

Other recent mailing address(es)

_____

_____

_____

_____

Financial

Financial Contacts

Financial Contacts at a Glance

List the main financial contacts in your life and their phone numbers (you'll add more details in the following pages). Bookmark this page so you can find it easily in the future.

ACCOUNTANT Name _____
        Phone Number _____

FINANCIAL ADVISOR Name _____
        Phone Number _____

Financial Contacts Worksheets

FINANCIAL	PERSONAL ACCOUNTANT
Firm Name:	
Accountant Name:	
Address:	
Telephone:	
Fax:	
Website:	
Email:	
Assistant Name:	
Assistant Telephone:	
Assistant Email:	
Notes:	

FINANCIAL — FINANCIAL ADVISOR

Firm Name:

Advisor Name:

Address:

Telephone:

Fax:

Website:

Email:

Assistant Name:

Assistant Telephone:

Assistant Email:

Notes:

ASSETS

Assets at a Glance

*Check if you have the item and know where the information is located.
Highlight or circle if you need to act on it. Cross it out if it's irrelevant to you. You
might also choose to include the monetary value of each asset.*

- ☐ Bank Account 1 _____
- ☐ Bank Account 2 _____
- ☐ Bank Account 3 _____
- ☐ Brokerage accounts _____
- ☐ Investments not with broker _____
- ☐ Annuities _____
- ☐ Real estate holdings _____
- ☐ Personal bonds _____
- ☐ Custodial accounts _____
- ☐ Pension plans _____
- ☐ Retirement plans _____
- ☐ 401K _____
- ☐ IRA (signify what type of IRA: Traditional, Rollover, Spousal, Roth, SEP) _____
- ☐ Education savings accounts or 529 plans _____
- ☐ Cash surrender of life insurance policies _____
- ☐ Other assets (gold, silver, collectables) _____
- ☐ Vehicle value _____
- ☐ Monies owed to you _____
- ☐ Additional assets _____

Assets Worksheets

FINANCIAL	BANK ACCOUNT 1
Bank Name:	
Account No.:	
Type of Account:	
Bank Contact:	
Branch Address:	
Banking Website:	
Username & Password: Telephone: Fax:	
Email:	
Notes:	

FINANCIAL	BANK ACCOUNT 2
Bank Name:	
Account No.:	
Type of Account:	
Bank Contact:	
Branch Address:	
Banking Website:	
Username & Password:	
Telephone:	
Fax:	
Email:	
Notes:	

FINANCIAL	BANK ACCOUNT 3
Bank Name:	
Account No.:	
Type of Account:	
Bank Contact:	
Branch Address:	
Banking Website:	
Username & Password:	
Telephone:	
Fax:	
Email:	
Notes:	

FINANCIAL	BROKERAGE ACCOUNT
Firm Name:	
Contact:	
Address:	
Telephone:	
Fax:	
Email:	
Website:	
Assistant Name:	
Assistant Telephone:	
Assistant Fax:	
Assistant Email:	
Notes:	

FINANCIAL	Investment Not with a Broker #1
Investment Name:	
Contact:	
Address:	
Telephone:	
Fax:	
Email:	
Notes:	

FINANCIAL	Investment Not with a Broker #2
Investment Name:	
Contact:	
Address:	
Telephone:	
Fax:	
Email:	
Notes:	

FINANCIAL	Annuity
Institution Name:	
Type of Account:	
Account Number:	
Contact:	
Address:	
Telephone:	
Email:	
Notes:	

FINANCIAL	Real Estate Holding #1
Property Name:	
Property Address:	
Contact:	
Address:	
Telephone:	
Fax:	
Email:	
Notes:	

FINANCIAL	Real Estate Holding #2
Property Name:	
Property Address:	
Contact:	
Address:	
Telephone:	
Fax:	
Email:	
Notes:	

FINANCIAL	Personal Bond
Name:	
Contact:	
Address:	
Telephone:	
Fax:	
Email:	
Notes:	

FINANCIAL	Custodial Account
Institution Name:	
Account Name:	
Account Number:	
Contact:	
Address:	
Telephone:	
Fax:	
Email:	
Notes:	

FINANCIAL	Pension Plan
Name of Plan:	
Type of Plan:	
Plan ID Number:	
Contact:	
Address:	
Telephone:	
Fax:	
Email:	
Notes:	

FINANCIAL	Retirement Plan
Name of Plan:	
Account Name:	
Account ID Number:	
Institution:	
Contact:	
Address:	
Telephone:	
Fax:	
Email:	
Notes:	

FINANCIAL	401K
Institution Name:	
Account Name:	
Account Number:	
Contact:	
Address:	
Telephone:	
Fax:	
Email:	
Notes:	

FINANCIAL   IRA

Institution Name:

Account Name:

Account Number:

Contact:

Address:

Telephone:

Fax:

Email:

Notes:

FINANCIAL   Education Savings

Institution Name:

Account Name:

Account Number:

Beneficiary:

Contact:

Address:

Telephone:

Fax:

Email:

Notes:

FINANCIAL	Cash Surrender of Life Insurance Policies
Policy Name:	
Policy Number:	
Contact:	
Address:	
Telephone:	
Fax:	
Email:	
Notes:	

FINANCIAL	Other Assets (Gold, Silver, Collectables)
Item(s):	
Held At:	
Appraisal Contact:	
Address:	
Telephone:	
Fax:	
Email:	
Notes:	

FINANCIAL	Vehicle 1
Make:	
Year:	
Model:	
VIN:	
Notes:	

FINANCIAL	Vehicle 2
Make:	
Year:	
Model:	
VIN:	
Notes:	

FINANCIAL	Monies Owed to You
Debtor Name:	
Address:	
Telephone:	
Fax:	
Email:	
Notes:	

FINANCIAL	Additional Assets
Describe #1:	
Notes:	
Describe #2:	
Notes:	
Describe #3:	
Notes:	

Insurance & Other Policies

Policies at a Glance

Check if you have the item and know where the information is located. Highlight or circle if you need to act on it. Cross it out if it's irrelevant to you. You might also choose to include the monetary value of each policy.

- ☐ Life insurance policy 1 _____
- ☐ Life insurance policy 2 _____
- ☐ Long-term care insurance policy _____
- ☐ Health and Rx insurance _____
- ☐ Casualty insurance policy_____
- ☐ Personal insurance policy _____
- ☐ Umbrella insurance policy _____
- ☐ Property insurance policy _____
- ☐ Mortgage insurance policy _____
- ☐ Valuables (art, jewelry, silverware) insurance policy _____
- ☐ Travel insurance policy _____
- ☐ Automobile insurance policy _____
- ☐ Other vehicle insurance policy _____
- ☐ Veterans Administration policy _____
- ☐ Military benefits or military survivor benefits policy _____
- ☐ Credit card or bank-sponsored policy _____
- ☐ Association-sponsored policy _____
- ☐ Employer or union-sponsored policy _____

Policies Worksheets

FINANCIAL	Life Insurance Policy No. 1
Company Name:	
Insured:	
Policy Number:	
Date of Birth:	
Policy Owner:	
Beneficiaries:	1. 2. 3.
Agent Name:	
Telephone:	
Fax:	
Email:	
Website:	
Username & Password:	
Notes:	

FINANCIAL	Life Insurance Policy No. 2
Company Name:	
Insured:	
Policy Number:	
Date of Birth:	
Policy Owner:	
Beneficiaries:	1.
	2.
	3.
Agent Name:	
Telephone:	
Fax:	
Email:	
Website:	
Username & Password:	
Notes:	

FINANCIAL	Long-Term Care Insurance Policy
Company Name:	
Policy Number:	
Name on Policy:	
Date of Birth:	
Agent Name:	
Telephone:	
Fax:	
Email:	
Website:	
Username & Password:	
Notes:	

FINANCIAL	Health Insurance —Primary Policy
Company Name:	
Policy Number:	
Name on Policy:	
Date of Birth:	
Contact Name:	
Telephone:	
Fax:	
Email:	
Website:	
Username & Password:	
Notes:	

FINANCIAL	Health Insurance — Secondary or Rx Policy
Company Name:	
Policy Number:	
Name on Policy:	
Date of Birth:	
Contact Name:	
Telephone:	
Fax:	
Email:	
Website:	
Username & Password:	
Notes:	

FINANCIAL — Casualty Insurance Policy

Company Name:

Policy Number:

Name on Policy:

Date of Birth:

Agent Name:

Telephone:

Fax:

Email:

Website:

Username & Password:

Notes:

FINANCIAL — Personal Insurance Policy

Company Name:

Policy Number:

Name on Policy:

Date of Birth:

Agent Name:

Telephone:

Fax:

Email:

Website:

Username & Password:

Notes:

FINANCIAL	Umbrella Insurance Policy
Company Name:	
Policy Number:	
Name on Policy:	
Date of Birth:	
Agent Name:	
Telephone:	
Fax:	
Email:	
Website:	
Username & Password:	
Notes:	

FINANCIAL	Property Insurance Policy #1
Company Name:	
Location of Property:	
Policy Number:	
Name on Policy:	
Date of Birth:	
Agent Name:	
Telephone:	
Fax:	
Email:	
Website:	
Username & Password:	
Notes:	

FINANCIAL	Property Insurance Policy #2
Company Name:	
Location of Property:	
Policy Number:	
Name on Policy:	
Date of Birth:	
Agent Name:	
Telephone:	
Fax:	
Email:	
Website:	
Username & Password:	
Notes:	

FINANCIAL	Mortgage Insurance Policy
Company Name:	
Location of Property:	
Policy Number:	
Names on Policy:	
Dates of Birth:	
Beneficiaries:	1.
	2.
	3.
Agent Name:	
Telephone:	
Fax:	
Email:	
Website:	
Username & Password:	
Notes:	

FINANCIAL	Valuables (Art, Jewelry, Silverware) Insurance Policy
Company Name:	
Policy Number:	
Name on Policy:	
Date of Birth:	
Agent Name:	
Telephone:	
Fax:	
Email:	
Website:	
Username & Password:	
Notes:	

FINANCIAL	Travel Insurance Policy
Company Name:	
Policy Number:	
Name on Policy:	
Date of Birth:	
Beneficiaries:	1.
	2.
	3.
Agent Name:	
Telephone:	
Fax:	
Email:	
Website:	
Username & Password:	
Notes:	

FINANCIAL	Automobile Insurance Policy
Company Name:	
Policy Number:	
Type of Vehicle:	
Identification Number:	
Name on Policy:	
Date of Birth:	
Contact Name:	
Telephone:	
Fax:	
Email:	
Website:	
Username & Password:	
Notes:	

FINANCIAL	Other Vehicle Insurance Policy
Company Name:	
Vehicle Description	
Identification Number:	
Policy Number:	
Name on Policy:	
Date of Birth:	
Contact Name:	
Telephone:	
Fax:	
Email:	
Website:	
Username & Password:	
Notes:	

FINANCIAL	Veterans Administration Policy
Company Name:	
Policy Number:	
Name on Policy:	
Date of Birth:	
Beneficiaries:	1.
	2.
	3.
Contact Name:	
Telephone:	
Fax:	
Email:	
Website:	
Username & Password:	
Notes:	

FINANCIAL	Military Benefits or Military Survivor Benefits Policy
Company Name:	
Policy Number:	
Name on Policy:	
Date of Birth:	
Beneficiaries:	1.
	2.
	3.
Contact Name:	
Telephone:	
Fax:	
Email:	
Website:	
Username & Password:	
Notes:	

FINANCIAL	Credit Card or Bank-Sponsored Policy
Company Name:	
Policy Number:	
Name on Policy:	
Date of Birth:	
Beneficiaries:	1.
	2.
	3.
Contact Name:	
Telephone:	
Fax:	
Email:	
Website:	
Username & Password:	
Notes:	

FINANCIAL	Association-Sponsored Policy
Company Name:	
Policy Number:	
Name on Policy:	
Date of Birth:	
Beneficiaries:	1. 2. 3.
Contact Name:	
Telephone:	
Fax:	
Email:	
Website:	
Username & Password:	
Notes:	

FINANCIAL	Employer or Union-Sponsored Policy
Company Name:	
Policy Number:	
Name on Policy:	
Date of Birth:	
Beneficiaries:	1.
	2.
	3.
Contact Name:	
Telephone:	
Fax:	
Email:	
Website:	
Username & Password:	
Notes:	

Liabilities

Liabilities at a Glance

Check if you have the item and know where the information is located. Highlight or circle if you need to act on it. Cross it out if it's irrelevant to you. To get a clear picture of your finances, you should add the amounts for each item.

- ☐ Mortgage _____
- ☐ Bank loan _____
- ☐ Line of credit _____
- ☐ Other loan _____
- ☐ Credit card 1 _____
- ☐ Credit card 2 _____
- ☐ Credit card 3 _____
- ☐ Auto loan _____
- ☐ Association fees _____
- ☐ Unpaid taxes _____
- ☐ Outstanding bills _____
- ☐ Eldercare obligations _____
- ☐ Alimony _____
- ☐ Childcare support _____
- ☐ Renter agreement _____
- ☐ Utility bills _____
- ☐ Additional liabilities/payables _____

Liabilities Worksheets

FINANCIAL	Mortgage
Company Name:	
Property Address:	
Policy Number:	
Name on Policy:	
Date of Birth:	
Contact Name:	
Telephone:	
Fax:	
Email:	
Notes:	

FINANCIAL	Bank Loan
Bank Name:	
Loan Number:	
Branch:	
Type of Loan:	
Contact Name:	
Telephone:	
Fax:	
Email:	
Notes:	

FINANCIAL	Line of Credit
Bank Name:	
Policy Number:	
Branch:	
Name on Policy:	
Date of Birth:	
Contact Name:	
Telephone:	
Fax:	
Email:	
Notes:	

FINANCIAL — Other Loan

Company Name:

Policy Number:

Name on Policy:

Date of Birth:

Contact Name:

Telephone:

Fax:

Email:

Notes:

FINANCIAL — Credit Card 1

Company Name:

Name on Card:

Card Number:

Security Number:

Telephone:

Fax:

Email:

Notes:

FINANCIAL	Credit Card 2
Company Name:	
Name on Card:	
Card Number:	
Security Number:	
Telephone:	
Fax:	
Email:	
Notes:	

FINANCIAL	Credit Card 3
Company Name:	
Name on Card:	
Card Number:	
Security Number:	
Telephone:	
Fax:	
Email:	
Notes:	

FINANCIAL — Auto Loan

Institution Name:

Policy Number:

Vehicle Description:

Identification Number:

Name on Policy:

Date of Birth:

Contact Name:

Telephone:

Fax:

Email:

Notes:

FINANCIAL — Association Fees

Association Name:

Contact Name:

Telephone:

Fax:

Email:

Notes:

FINANCIAL	Unpaid Taxes
Government Department:	
Type of Tax:	
Identification Number:	
Name	
Date of Birth:	
Contact Name:	
Telephone:	
Fax:	
Email:	
Notes:	

FINANCIAL — Outstanding Bills

Company Name:

Type and Description:

Name on Bill:

Identification Number:

Contact Name:

Telephone:

Fax:

Email:

Notes:

FINANCIAL	Eldercare Obligations
Company Name:	
Type and Description:	
Name:	
Date of Birth:	
Contact Name:	
Telephone:	
Fax:	
Email:	
Notes:	

FINANCIAL	Alimony
Money Due To:	
Agreement:	
Date of Birth:	
Contact Name:	
Telephone:	
Fax:	
Email:	
Notes:	

FINANCIAL — Childcare Support

Payable To:

Names of children:

Dates of Birth:

Contact:

Telephone:

Fax:

Email:

Notes:

FINANCIAL — Renter Agreement

Name of Lessor:

Property Address:

Contact Person:

Contact Address:

Telephone:

Fax:

Email:

Notes:

FINANCIAL	Additional Liabilities/Payables
Payable To:	
Description:	
Contact Name:	
Telephone:	
Fax:	
Email:	
Notes:	

Legal & Estate

Legal & Estate Contacts at a Glance

General attorney   Name _____

Phone Number _____

Estate attorney   Name _____

Phone Number _____

Legal & Estate Contacts Worksheet

LEGAL	Attorney 1
Firm Name:	
Attorney Name:	
Address:	
Telephone:	
Fax:	
Email:	
Assistant Name:	
Assistant Telephone:	
Assistant Email:	
Notes:	

LEGAL	Attorney 2
Firm Name:	
Attorney Name:	
Address:	
Telephone:	
Fax:	
Email:	
Assistant Name:	
Assistant Telephone:	
Assistant Email:	
Notes:	

Legal & Estate Documents at a Glance

Check if you have the item and know where the information is located. Highlight or circle if you need to act on it. Cross it out if it's irrelevant to you.

☐ **Current will**

    Location: _____

☐ **Trust** (family, charitable, estate, revocable, irrevocable)

    Location: _____

☐ **Guardianship of minors**

    Location: _____

☐ **Living will**

    Location: _____

☐ **Durable power of attorney**

    Location: _____

☐ **Medical power of attorney**

    Location: _____

☐ **Prenuptual agreement**

    Location: _____

☐ **Domestic partner agreement**

    Location: _____

☐ **Family partnership agreement**

Location: _____

☐ **Cohabitation agreement**

Location: _____

☐ **Post-nuptual agreement**

Location: _____

☐ **Child support agreement**

Location: _____

☐ **Deeds**

Location: _____

☐ **Health care directive**

Location: _____

☐ **Estate documents**

Location: _____

☐ **Property titles and deeds**

Location: _____

☐ **Real estate documents**

Location: _____

☐ **Investment documents**

Location: _____

Business

If you (or the person for whom you're filling out this information) is currently employed, self-employed, or a business owner, it's important to keep track of certain pieces of professional information. If you work for a company, I've provided a simple checklist, which includes items you should have. You should also know where they are located. This is Section A.

If you are self-employed or own a business, in addition to those checklists, I've added more extensive worksheets and contact information. This is Section B.

Of course, as with all of Part Two, some of these things may not apply to your particular situation, while other items may be missing. Complete the necessary sections and include additional details using the blank pages at the end of this section.

SECTION A

Employment Information at a Glance

Check if you have the item and know where the information is located.
Highlight or circle if you need to act on it. Cross it out if it's irrelevant to you.

☐ Company name: _____

☐ Company address: _____

☐ Company telephone number: _____

☐ Company general email address: _____

☐ Main contact: _____

☐ Other contacts: _____

☐ Employer retirement plan(s)
   Location: _____

☐ Workers compensation plan
   Location: _____

☐ Other benefit plans
   Location: _____

☐ Union affiliation
   Location: _____

☐ Professional associations
   Location: _____

SECTION B

Business Owner Contacts at a Glance

BUSINESS ACCOUNTANT

Name _____

Phone Number _____

BUSINESS ATTORNEY

Name _____

Phone Number _____

BUSINESS ADVISOR

Name _____

Phone Number _____

BUSINESS — Business Accountant

Firm Name:

Attorney Name:

Address:

Telephone:

Fax:

Email:

Assistant Name:

Assistant Telephone:

Assistant Email:

Notes:

BUSINESS — Business Attorney

Firm Name:

Attorney Name:

Address:

Telephone:

Fax:

Email:

Assistant Name:

Assistant Telephone:

Assistant Email:

Notes:

BUSINESS	Business Advisor
Firm Name:	
Advisor Name:	
Address:	
Telephone:	
Fax:	
Email:	
Assistant Name:	
Assistant Telephone:	
Assistant Email:	
Notes:	

Business Owner Information at a Glance

Check if you have the item and know where the information is located. Highlight or circle if you need to act on it. Cross it out if it's irrelevant to you.

☐ Business computer info
Location: _____

☐ Business electronics (other)
Location: _____

☐ Employees
Location: _____

☐ Business license(s)
Location: _____

☐ Business bank account(s)
Location: _____

☐ Business investment(s)
Location: _____

☐ Disability insurance
Location: _____

☐ Workers Compensation Insurance
Location: _____

☐ Partners insurance
Location: _____

☐ Property insurance
Location: _____

☐ Other business insurance

Location: _____

☐ Business records

Location: _____

☐ Articles of incorporation

Location: _____

☐ Operating agreements

Location: _____

☐ Key business contacts

Location: _____

☐ Buy/sell agreement

Location: _____

☐ Professional associations

Location: _____

☐ Real estate

Location: _____

☐ Leases (auto, space)

Location: _____

☐ Tax records

Location: _____

☐ Business debt

Location: _____

Business Worksheets

BUSINESS	Computer Info
Item:	
Manufacturer:	
Model and Year:	
Serial Number:	
Technician Name:	
Telephone:	
Email:	
Notes:	

BUSINESS	Other Electronics
Item:	
Manufacturer:	
Model and Year:	
Serial Number:	
Technician Name:	
Telephone:	
Email:	
Notes:	

BUSINESS	Employees
Company Name:	
Number of Employees:	
Location of Personnel Files:	
Company Address:	
Telephone:	
Fax:	
Email:	
Notes:	

BUSINESS	Business License #1
Company Name:	
Type of License:	
Contact Name:	
Telephone:	
Fax:	
Email:	
Notes:	

BUSINESS	Business License #2
Company Name:	
Type of License:	
Contact Name:	
Telephone:	
Fax:	
Email:	
Notes:	

BUSINESS	Business License #3
Company Name:	
Type of License:	
Contact Name:	
Telephone:	
Fax:	
Email:	
Notes:	

BUSINESS	Business Bank Account #1
Bank Name:	
Branch:	
Address:	
Type of Account:	
Account Number:	
Contact Name:	
Telephone:	
Fax:	
Banking Website:	
Username & Password:	
Email:	
Notes:	

BUSINESS — Business Bank Account #2

Bank Name:

Branch:

Address:

Type of Account:

Account Number:

Contact Name:

Telephone:

Fax:

Banking Website:

Username & Password:

Email:

Notes:

BUSINESS	Business Investment
Institution/Firm Name:	
Type of Investment:	
Name on Agreement:	
Contact Name:	
Telephone:	
Fax:	
Email:	
Notes:	

BUSINESS	Disability Insurance
Company Name:	
Policy Number:	
Name on Policy:	
Date of Birth:	
Agent Name:	
Telephone:	
Fax:	
Email:	
Notes:	

BUSINESS	Workers Compensation Insurance
Company Name:	
Policy Number:	
Name on Policy:	
Date of Birth:	
Contact Name:	
Telephone:	
Fax:	
Email:	
Notes:	

BUSINESS	Partners Insurance
Company Name:	
Policy Number:	
Names on Policy:	
Beneficiaries:	1.
	2.
	3.
Contact Name:	
Telephone:	
Fax:	
Email:	
Notes:	

BUSINESS	Property Insurance
Company Name:	
Policy Number:	
Name on Policy:	
Location of Property:	
Contact Name:	
Telephone:	
Fax:	
Email:	
Notes:	

BUSINESS	Other Business Insurance
Company Name:	
Type of Insurance:	
Policy Number:	
Name on Policy:	
Date of Birth:	
Beneficiaries:	1.
	2.
	3.
Contact Name:	
Telephone:	
Fax:	
Email:	
Notes:	

BUSINESS	Business Records
Company Name:	
Location of Records:	
Accessible By:	
Telephone:	
Fax:	
Email:	
Notes:	

BUSINESS	Articles of Incorporation
Corporation Name:	
Date of Incorporation:	
Location:	
Contact Name:	
Telephone:	
Fax:	
Email:	
Notes:	

BUSINESS	Operating Agreements
Company Name:	
Type of Agreements:	
Location:	
Contact Name:	
Telephone:	
Fax:	
Email:	
Notes:	

BUSINESS	Key Business Contacts
Name	Contact Information
Notes	

BUSINESS	Buy/Sell Agreement
Company Name:	
Parties to Agreement:	
Location of Documents:	
Contact Name:	
Telephone:	
Fax:	
Email:	
Notes:	

BUSINESS	Professional Association
Name of Association:	
Membership ID:	
Contact Name:	
Telephone:	
Email:	
Website:	
Notes:	

BUSINESS	Real Estate Holding
Property Name:	
Property Address:	
Contact:	
Address:	
Telephone:	
Fax:	
Email:	
Notes:	

BUSINESS	Lease
Property Name:	
Property Address:	
Contact:	
Telephone:	
Fax:	
Email:	
Notes:	

BUSINESS	Business Debt
Name of Holder:	
Debt Type:	
Contact:	
Telephone:	
Email:	
Due date:	
Notes:	

Personal and Domestic Information

Personal and Domestic Contacts at a Glance

Check if you have the item and know where the information is located. Highlight or circle if you need to act on it. Cross it out if it's irrelevant to you.

☐ Clergy _____

☐ Primary Care Doctor _____

☐ Specialist(s) _____

PERSONAL	Clergy
Name of Institution:	
Name of Clergy:	
Address:	
Telephone:	
Fax:	
Email:	
Notes:	

PERSONAL	Primary Care Doctor
Name of Practice:	
Name of Doctor:	
Address:	
Telephone:	
Fax:	
Email:	
Notes:	

PERSONAL	Specialist #1
Name of Practice:	
Name of Doctor:	
Specialty:	
Address:	
Telephone:	
Fax:	
Email:	
Notes:	

PERSONAL — Specialist #2

Name of Practice:

Name of Doctor:

Specialty:

Address:

Telephone:

Fax:

Email:

Notes:

PERSONAL — Specialist #3

Name of Practice:

Name of Doctor:

Specialty:

Address:

Telephone:

Fax:

Email:

Notes:

PERSONAL	Specialist #4
Name of Practice:	
Name of Doctor:	
Specialty:	
Address:	
Telephone:	
Fax:	
Email:	
Notes:	

PERSONAL	Specialist #5
Name of Practice:	
Name of Doctor:	
Specialty:	
Address:	
Telephone:	
Fax:	
Email:	
Notes:	

Personal and Domestic Information at a Glance

Check if you have the item and know where the information is located. Highlight or circle if you need to act on it. Cross it out if it's irrelevant to you.

□ Social Security card
Location: _____

□ Passport/citizenship papers
Location: _____

□ TSA and Global Pass
Location: _____

□ Driver's license
Location: _____

□ Marriage certificate
Location: _____

□ Divorce decree
Location: _____

□ Separation agreement
Location: _____

□ Adoption papers
Location: _____

□ Military discharge papers
Location: _____

□ Postal box agreement
Location: _____

☐ **HOA**

Location: _____

☐ **List of medications**

Location: _____

☐ **Household service contracts and manuals**

Location: _____

☐ **List of service people**

Location: _____

☐ **Community organizations**

Location: _____

☐ **School leadership**

Location: _____

FINANCIAL	Location of Copies of Bills
Landline Telephone:	
Electricity:	
Gas:	
Water:	
Trash:	
Recycling:	
Cable TV:	
Satellite TV:	
Internet:	
Mobile Phone:	
Other:	
Other:	
Other:	

Caregiving

Caregiving Contacts at a Glance

Check if you have the item and know where the information is located. Highlight or circle if you need to act on it. Cross it out if it's irrelevant to you.

☐ Caregiving agency
Location: _____

☐ Employed caregivers
Location: _____

CAREGIVING	Caregiving Agency
Name of Agency:	
Location of Documents:	
Address:	
Contact Name:	
Telephone:	
Fax:	
Email:	
Notes:	

CAREGIVING	Employed Caregivers
Name of Caregiver:	
Location of Documents:	
Address:	
Telephone:	
Fax:	
Email:	
Notes:	

Caregiving Information at a Glance

Check if you have the item and know where the information is located. Highlight or circle if you need to act on it. Cross it out if it's irrelevant to you.

☐ Dependent care instructions
Location: _____

☐ Legal guardian information
Location: _____

End-of-Life Arrangements

End-of-Life Arrangements at a Glance

Check if you have the item and know where the information is located. Highlight or circle if you need to act on it. Cross it out if it's irrelevant to you.

- ☐ Funeral arrangements
  Location: _____

- ☐ Burial arrangements
  Location: _____

- ☐ Organ donation
  Location: _____

End-of-Life Worksheets

END-OF-LIFE	Funeral Arrangements
Contact Name:	
Location of Documents:	
Telephone:	
Fax:	
Email:	
Notes:	

END-OF-LIFE	Burial Arrangements
Mortuary Name:	
Location of Documents:	
Advisor:	
Address:	
Telephone:	
Fax:	
Email:	
Notes:	

For Additional Notes

For Additional Notes

For Additional Notes

For Additional Notes

When the Time Comes, What to Do First

"It does not matter how slowly you go
as long as you do not stop."

~ *Confucius*

The day will come when you—or your loved ones—will need all of the information you have written down in this book. When that day comes, the hard work you've done to become organized and prepared will help immensely, but you and/or your family will still feel lost and confused. There is no escaping the sadness of loss, and no book or amount of preparation can buffer you from it. This book is simply a tool to help you cope.

For that reason, I urge you to bookmark this section. Here, I will tell you exactly what you need to do and the order in which to do it. Let's start with the most important things.

First Hours and Days

In my speaking engagements, I am often asked what to do right away if someone dies. You might be fairly well prepared on paper, have your worksheets all filled out, and feel you have a strong roadmap about how to proceed. But during the initial shock, when you must react quickly, don't be surprised to find yourself befuddled.

Here, I've outlined the first steps to alleviate at least a little of the anxiety and wonderment. In those first minutes, hours, and days, you'll need someone telling you exactly what to do. I am honored to be that person.

Pronouncement of death

If the death occurred at home, call either 911, the local police non-emergency number, a hospice you've been working with, a coroner, or the family doctor. Choose the one that feels most comfortable to you. They will all know what to do.

Arrange for the body to be removed

I hope you have someone with you for support in this moment. It will be an emotional time. Generally, whomever you have called for the "pronouncement of death" will take care of this step for you. Your job is simply to get through it.

Notify family and friends

You can make the first few calls and then ask others to pass the information along. When you make those calls, don't be afraid to ask for help. Everyone who cares about you *wants* to do whatever they can to make this easier for you.

Burial and funeral arrangements

If you have completed the other tasks in this book so far, then you already know the deceased's wishes and plans, as well as whether he or she hoped to donate organs. You may be assigned a mortuary advisor. Meet with that person to review details, prepare an obituary and newspaper notices, secure death certificates (more on this below), and visit the mortuary. I highly recommend having a loved one with you throughout this process.

First-Priority Tasks

Notify your team

While the makeup of this team is different for every person, it will likely include a combination of attorneys, financial advisors, accountants, insurance agents, and other professional service providers. You can flip back to pages xx-xx for all of the relevant contact information for your unique situation. Ideally, you will have already introduced these people to each other. They can act as a team on your behalf. Now is the time for their teamwork to come together.

Life insurance

Notify your brokers so they can file claims for any payments you will be due and amend the policies that need to be changed.

Other types of insurance

You'll need to cancel or amend any other types of insurance policies you and your loved one may have, including automobile insurance, health insurance, long-term life insurance, and umbrella insurance. You can flip back to pages xx-xx for all of the relevant contact information.

Social Security

Notify the Social Security Administration of your loss immediately by calling (800) 772-1213. Note that some funeral homes do this for you, so check with them first. If and when you make the call, you will need:

- The deceased's Social Security number
- Date of birth
- Date of marriage (if applicable)

Social security will also give you a one-time benefit of $255 if you are a surviving spouse or child of the deceased. (Note that this amount may change in the future. Call Social Security for details.)

Federal benefits

If your spouse has been receiving federal benefits, such as Social Security or Medicare, and if you are old enough to receive those benefits, you are entitled to the larger amount: either 50 percent of your spouse's allowance or 100 percent of yours. To claim spousal benefits, you'll need a copy of your marriage certificate.

Second-Priority Tasks

In addition, there is a laundry list of tasks that must be completed immediately following a death. Many of these things can be delegated to loved ones, so do not resist the urge to hand this list off to someone else who is willing and eager to assist.

☐ Obtain multiple copies of the death certificate (the funeral home can help with this)

- ☐ Make copies of the dated obituary notice

- ☐ Make copies of any other relevant newspaper articles

- ☐ Review will and trust with attorney and proceed with filing

- ☐ Contact all banks and creditors and notify them of the death

- ☐ Meet with your accountant

- ☐ Check safe deposit box contents

- ☐ Make copies of marriage certificates

- ☐ Make copies of birth certificates (both yours and the deceased's)

- ☐ Compile a list of heirs, next of kin, and beneficiaries

- ☐ Check life insurance policies and contact them to file for benefits

- ☐ Locate military records and file for any veteran benefits

- ☐ File for any fraternal, union, or association benefits

- ☐ File for any employer benefits

- ☐ Check health insurance continuation policy for survivors

- ☐ Review your own will and make any necessary changes

- ☐ Pre-arrange your own post-mortem services, if you have not already

- ☐ Establish credit in your name

- ☐ Transfer the car title(s) into your name

Third-Priority Tasks

Once you've taken care of the above tasks, you can move on to the less-important task of cancelling accounts, subscriptions, etc., and in some cases, reinstating them in your own name. Below is a laundry list of types of accounts you may need to deal with. All of these examples may not apply to your situation, and there may be some I am missing. But hopefully, this will help you get started.

- Mobile device service (cell phones, iPads, Kindles)
- Social networks (Facebook, Instagram, Twitter, Google+, LinkedIn, Tumblr)
- Automobile registration (notify the DMV so you do not receive renewal and past-due notices in the future)
- Magazine and periodical subscriptions
- Email accounts
- Utilities in the deceased's name
- Professional and social memberships and listings
- Airline mileage accounts (usually, you can transfer your spouse's miles or points to your own name, if you have your own account with the same airline)
- Mailing lists (alumni groups, charitable organizations)

Direct mail and telemarketing lists: call the national credit reporting agencies' opt-out line at (888) 567-8688 to reduce unsolicited offers from credit cards; contact the Direct Marketing Association at http://www.dmachoice.org or call (212) 382-1222 to get off telemarketing lists; contact the Do Not Call Registry at http://www.donotcall.gov or (888) 382-1222.

DISCLAIMER: Susan Alpert has, to the best of her ability, verified the accuracy of all information and advice within this book. As with all tax and financial recommendations, please check with your attorney, accountant, and other members of your professional team for the current laws and processes applicable to your state.

"What we think or what we know or what we believe is, in the end, of little consequence. The only consequence is what we do."

~ John Ruskin

Acknowledgements

I always wondered why authors had so many people to acknowledge in the collaboration of a book. The elements that comprise the finished product are so much more than just the words between the covers, and the people who play a part in getting a book to market are invaluable. It would be impossible to list the many who were influences in the creation of "Later is Too Late", but I hope you know who you are and how much I appreciate and applaud you.

Kudos to all the women who so graciously shared their personal stories with me, so I in turn could present them to you. My editors Joslyn McIntyre and Taylor Mallory lived through the venture with amazing patience, as did Patty King, my creative graphic designer. My thanks and gratitude to Joanne Black, Allen Kardell and Merle Tabor Stern for their eagle eyes and early input, and to John Stillman and Carol Schaner for their professional advice. The encouragement and understanding of my family and friends made the journey worthwhile.

Made in the USA
San Bernardino, CA
05 May 2016